Economics for Everyone
Das Jus Kapital

Philip McShane

Axial Press Inc
Halifax

The diagrams from Robert Gordon, *Macroeconomics*, 6th edition, 1993
are reproduced by permission of Addison-Wesley Educational
Publishers, Inc. Quotations from unpublished economic writings
of Bernard Lonergan are printed by permission of the Trustees of
the Bernard Lonergan Estate.

Printed in Canada.

Axial Press Inc
PO Box 2584 CRO
Halifax, Nova Scotia
B3J 3N5 Canada
axialpress@istar.ca
http://home.istar.ca/~axial

Lonergan
HB
171
.M37
1998
cp. 2

Canadian Cataloguing in Publication Data

McShane, Philip, 1932-
    Economics for everyone : Das Jus Kapital

2nd ed.
Includes bibliographical references.
ISBN 0-9684503-1-8

    1. Economics. 2. Distributive justice. I. Title.

HB171.M32 1998   330   C99-900012-8

To my wife, Sally

A single copy of a book, transplanted by
chance and fallen upon a mind that was
receptive ground for that particular way of
feeling, is enough to introduce to a patch of
ground a plant that did not previously exist
and that suddenly thrives and overruns it.

André Maurois
From Proust to Camus
Doubleday Anchor, 1968, 8

Contents

TRANSAXIAL SERIES
A Series Within Axial Press

Editor's Introduction

Some $4 trillion in institutional capital, blown around the
world by the fickle wings of investor psychology, builds up
into huge waves, which can produce fantastic rates of
growth. But those waves also can produce big bubbles.[1]

It may seem strange to find a quotation from a current *Time* at the
beginning of an editorial purportedly dealing with the long axial
period of fragmentation and disorientation that gives this press and
this series their names. Yet the problem that Eugene Linden points
to here is deeply axial in our sense, the sense sketched in the first
book of the series.[2] Briefly there is a long period – think of 5000
years, reaching to the middle of the new millennium – in which
human life has driven forward *speculatively* towards fragmentation
and disorientation, and one might say that bubbles of speculative
investment have been increasingly with us during that period. To
reach forward out of the mode, mood, muddle, of that disorientation, with some efficiency of self-taste, is to be transaxial. In that
sense I would claim that the distant solution offered by this small
book is transaxial.

1 Eugene Linden, "Volatility: Get Used To It", *Time*, September 28, 1998, 53.
2 Philip McShane, Editor's Introduction and end of chapter one, 38-48, *A Brief
History of Tongue . From Big Bang to Coloured Wholes*, Axial Press, Halifax, 1998.

It is transaxial in its content, in its presentation, and in its hopelessness. A few words on each of these aspects of the work should help you to glimpse what you are getting into here.

First, the book is transaxial in its drive towards an answer to the question, What is money? The conclusion of chapter one points to the failure of Galbraith even to raise that question properly. Raising it properly plunges one into the discomforting task of real economic analysis, something quite absent from the present theoretic bent. But my extravagant claim, for conventional economists altogether ridiculous, plunges us into deep water. The only sensible way forward now is to tackle chapter one. But perhaps a little ramble into the history of medicine would help you towards an axial glimpse.

Our past century has developed a rather sophisticated view, and related complex practices, regarding the circulation of blood, inside and outside the body. We are now a long way, in most cultures, from *Hirudo medicinalis*, the medicinal leech. And we are increasingly cautious about transfusions.

What is blood? It is an aggregate of circulating components that pertain to the health of the organism. Roughly, red cells oxygenate, white cells repair, platelets coagulate. Correspondingly, there are illnesses: red flow shrinkage breeds anemia; white flow can oscillate into leukemia or leukopenia; platelet disorder can have the modesty of an aspirin intake or the massiveness of thrombosis. Details are not relevant here: my point is that these distinctions and related practices are part of our culture. Relevant advances in understanding have led to common talk and acceptable practices. Hospital staff may have slight understanding of the chemistry of leukemia and anemia, but leeches are normally out.

In the economy there are three fundamental components of circulation, to be described in elementary fashion in chapter three. There is, if you like, the red flow of consumer circulation; there is the white flow of repair and replacement of production goods; there is the platelet pattern of a redistrubutive creative inhibition of clotting. Sometime in the next millennium the precisions of Schumpeter and Lonergan and Kalecki regarding these functions and their control will be common talk, a common ethos. Random transfusions of government blood and the casinos of economic leeching will be identified, ridiculed, abhorred, in their unintelligent destructive ugliness. Linden's article has the heading "Volatility: Get Used To It". The issue, however, is not volatility but voodoo. It is a voodoo that is, of course, well-dressed and well-spoken, but its talk of taxation and tuning and turn-ups takes sound bites out of the heart of progress.

Within that axial voodoo talk there is a pattern of educational talk which guarantees its persistent betrayal of our humanness. It is the talk I speak of in chapter one, when I deal with a standard presentation of economics. It is not quest-echoing speech, but the dull rot of rote. So, there is a transaxial lift of presentation in the book that is best recognized in its respect for slow growth.

Such respect belongs to pre-axial consciousness. The elder woman repeats the tribal tale freshly to fire-lit faces. It is reached for with a boned patience that may carry youth to adult appreciation and to elder tribal wisdom. Here, Hear: in a sentence we skim past characters of our axial age, teachers who tell no tale but trivialize us with so-called definitions. That trivialization is as close to your bones as those forgotten definitions, which were, after all, only longer names for the same neglected puzzle, puzzling: *circle?*, *locus of coplanar points equidistant from a fixed point?*, *interest rate?*, ...?[3]

We live in an encyclopedic age donated to us by the web of enlightenment. In that age the slick summary is sacred, and first-year university courses are designed to fix us in the essentials.[4] But essentials, appreciations, are distant goals. What one gets from the regular

3 You may fill in the blank from some regular textbook. If, however, you are interested in reaching some serious glimpse of the realities, I suggest that you try chapter five of Joseph Schumpeter's neglected little book, *The Theory of Economic Development*, first published in German in 1911. The English translation appeared in 1934 published by Oxford University Press, New York.
4 Joan Robinson describes crisply such fixity in the question of the measurement of capital. See page 21 below.

bad first year course – in economics, psychology, whatever – are slogans and misfit formulae. What one gets from a good first year course is a beginning. Getting beyond the well-dressed farce of present academic initiation is a massive transaxial task and *evidently* the task cannot be described here. Perhaps the end of chapter one and the beginning of chapter five will tempt you to climb towards *evidence*?

This little book, then, is only a beginning. What moves, heats, cools, the sun, the stars, the galaxies? Well, let's start with the moon going round the earth. What moves, heats, cools, the local and global markets? Well, let's start with one small island and one disturbed market. Only later, in growing lucid appreciation, can one move to the meaning of credit, interest rates, laws of return, redistributive transactions, etc. And one then has the chance to become not just an old bore, but an elder bower of wisdom.

The chance? It is dominated, in our times, by probability distributions of rare events. So we arrive at my axial hopelessness. It is neatly symbolized for me in the recent emergence of a likely replacement for Samuelson's axial text. In the Introduction to *For a New Political Economy*[5] I drew attention to the challenge of replacing that tradition, and now – thank-you, Mankiw (which rhymes with thank-you) – we have a replacement, not at all what I wished, but basically the same old same old.[6] Obviously, the end of an editorial is no place for a book review. However, the question on which I focused – What is money? – turns up in section 27.1, pretty late in the book and it is treated with brutal triviality.[7] This titanic needs an

5 B. Lonergan, *For A New Political Economy*, ed. P. McShane, University of Toronto Press, Toronto, 1999, xxxi.
6 Gregory Mankiw, *Principles of Economics*, Dryden Press, 1998.
7 To reach an adequate perspective on the meaning of money one might follow up the index entries under *Concomitance* in the work cited in footnote 5.

iceberg, but at present it is voyaging comfortably round the universities of the United States with every sign of corrupting young minds for decades to come.[8] In the face of the utter mess of the world economy, the band plays on. The melodies are tunes of financial fictions with no real economic analysis on board.

So, we move into the new millennium with no sign of serious blood counting, white or red. Thrombosis rules the daze.

Recently, Eugene Linden, whom I quoted at the beginning, wrote a book entitled *The Future in Plain Sight*.[9] He gives in it sound clues to expected instabilities that enlarge on the solid thrust of his *Time* essay. For me, however, the future is not in plain sight: but there is the seed in our miseries and in our desires and in our deeper drive for genuine science that would lift us quite beyond our present dull tolerance of trivial economic pursuits. In my transaxial hope, beyond my axial hopelessness, *the future is not what it was*.[10]

PHILIP MᶜSHANE

8 Bernard Lonergan used to tell the joke about Samuelson not changing his mind because he was making so much money from his text. The publishers advanced $1.4 million to Mankiw and will, no doubt, push against my Hebrew hope. What chance has Lonergan's David shot got against this Goliath?
9 Simon and Schuster, 1998.
10 See the conclusion of chapter five.

Prologue

The title of this small book has various meanings. The most evident meaning is that the book makes economics available to the common reader, and this is my primary meaning. Indeed, for reasons that will appear, I expect the common reader to make more sense of it than the sophisticated economist. I am presenting here a theory, view, of the proper workings of national and global economics which I might claim to be shockingly obvious yet also shockingly absent from the minds of economists.

The second meaning of the title is that economics is democratic, for everyone in that sense. This would seem part of the obvious, and perhaps most economists and politicians would claim that this is their view of economic activity. Yet there is a sense in which the obvious workings of present economies, even in the so-called free democratic world, are for the benefit of the controllers of money and management, with a sort of fallout that benefits the middleclass and the meek.

A third meaning, then, lurks in my title. It is that the control of the economy is for the many, and furthermore that it is not essentially a political issue. A parallel will help here, and indeed it is a parallel which I will exploit throughout the book. The control of driving the standard car is certainly in the hands of the many, and certainly is not an area of political debate. There is a right way to get a gear-shift automobile to move and to accelerate. It is not a topic for parliament. What can be a topic for public debate is the use and abuse of the travel-potential that the automobile represents, the manner in which this structures inner cities and outer linkages, etc.

These last sentences could well be a source of confusion to you, which surely would be a pity at this early stage of what claims to be a popularly enlightening book. So we need to pause over the parallel I am drawing between driving an automobile and the 'driving' of the economy. The precise parallel draws on the fact that an automobile has norms of driving built into it: there are rhythms in which you press the accelerator, use the clutch, change gear, brake. If you go against these norms of driving then you fail to drive the car properly, indeed you may damage the engine. The parallel emerges in the claim that the economy has norms of *driving* built into it. Helping you discover, in some elementary fashion, what these norms are, will occupy us for most of this book. I will only say two things about them here before going on with my description of the parallel.

First of all, these norms are not the familiar stuff of traditional economic texts, and I suspect that my book will be less comprehensible to people versed in that tradition, be they undergraduates or professors, than to people who are innocent of present economics. Secondly, glimpsing the norms within the rhythms of the productions and innovations of economic processes is going to take a fair amount of concrete imagination. The norms I write of, then, are not familiar to either type of reader. So, I must ask you at this stage to bear with me as I draw out my parallel.

I ask you, then, to accept provisionally my hypothesis that there are rhythms within a properly functioning economy, national or global. What I mean by properly-functioning is, of course, tied in with the as-yet unspecified normativity: something parallel to 'don't press on the brake and the accelerator at the same time'. If you accept that there is such a parallel between car and economy, then you can accept that it is possible to claim that 'the economy is being badly driven'. Such a claim, needless to say, is common enough to us: lay-persons and economists alike criticize government policies.

But what I hope to move you towards in this book is a notion and a competence, not of criticizing government, but of self-criticism of citizens.

For this we need a twist on our parallel. Normally, one citizen drives each car. If the driving is poor or appalling, this is pretty evident to citizens in the vicinity, especially if they are in the back seat or within striking distance. Even if only to avoid being considered incompetent or being arrested, citizens drive their cars fairly well: my reader will, no doubt, be able to smile over the accepted meaning of *fairly well* in, say, Montreal, Rome, or Bombay. But within any particular community there is a pressure of accepted common meaning inviting, cajoling, forcing, a certain competence.

What my parallel looks to, and the book seeks to make plausible, is the development of a like common meaning in the citizens of the world regarding the driving of the economy. The shrewd, well-informed reader may well pause here to suspect that what I am talking about cannot be some centralized imposed decision: monetary policy, taxation, interest rate.[1] What happens to these in the analysis we are undertaking is a later topic. But, no, I am not talking about some blind acceptance of a bank-rate: I am talking about a common view of proper economic driving that is prior to bank-rates or taxation policies. I am talking about a genuine democracy of minding the economy. Obviously, then, I am writing of something remote, and I risk recalling here the title of an article I wrote on the topic twenty years ago: "An Improbable Christian Vision and

---

1 Adolf Lowe stresses the need for 'Control', the root of all standard solutions to economic problems. See his *On Economic Knowledge. Towards a Science of Political Economy*, Harper and Row, NY, 1965; *The Path of Economic Growth*, Cambridge University Press, 1976. In contrast to *control* there is *microautonomy*, the distant democratic goal of the present view. See P. McShane, *Wealth of Self and Wealth of Nations, Self-Axis of the Great Ascent*, University Press of America, 1978, chapter 10, second edition, Axial Press, forthcoming.

the Economic Rhythms of the Second Million Years."[2] Here I am not writing about a Christian vision of the economy, no more than I am writing about a Christian vision of the automobile. I am writing about an intelligent attitude towards natural rhythms, about such an attitude gradually entering the minds and bones of citizens. Gradually? I write with a very long-term optimism. I envisage a distant future when the ethos of driving the economy properly will have the same character as the present ethos of car-driving. At present, all the citizens in advance nations may learn to drive some automobile in a complex culture of car-movements. In that future time, all the citizens might learn to drive a single economy in a culture concretely supportive of the rhythms of economic progress.

Such a shift of perspective is not to be expected in these decades. Bernard Lonergan, the thinker who originated the view I am attempting to popularize, remarked to me once, "this is going to take 150 years."[3] Why he picked that number I can only surmise. Certainly it is a larger pessimism than that of Max Planck, who hoped that his views in physics would be accepted when older professors died. But then there is much more at stake in present economic mismanagement, and there is an arrogant solidarity at the end of this century in economic theory that was not matched by the physics community at its beginning. One dissenting economic voice of these past decades, Alfred Eichner, has regularly expressed his conviction about the tightly structured clique that holds present and future economic education by the throat, but he adds a touch of hopeful humour when he remarks:

2 The title of chapter 6 of P. McShane, *Lonergan's Challenge to the University and the Economy*, University Press of America, 1981. Chapter 7 contrasts Lonergan's economics with contemporary views.

3 The remark was made in the Autumn of 1977, when I was assisting Lonergan in preparation for his first course of lectures on Economics, Spring 1978, in Boston College Theology Department. I had presented the theory in a Workshop there in the Summer of 1977.

Late in the day, after they have had two or three drinks, many economic professors will begin to admit to their own reservations about the theory which forms the core of the economics curriculum. The theory, they will acknowledge, is at odds with much that is known about the behaviour of economic institutions. 'But what else is there to teach our students?' they will ask.[4]

Perhaps introductory economics should be taught late in the evening!

In the present sad state of economic science certainly there is room for humour and satire. One of my shots at the like, in these past decades of popular presentations, has been to compare the economist to a driver who, stupidly, ignorant of standard driving, pushes along in a single gear, and when the engine overheats, decides to get the car painted. An image you may find more telling, perhaps, is to envisage economists as people on a beach trying to make the tide come in flat or in a steady slope. The latter image hits off very nicely the silly going-against-nature that, I would claim, is part and parcel of traditional equilibrium theory or, its first cousin, steady growth theory. But I am touching here on larger topics that would only distract my interested beginner. So I cut short my diversion into current economics with a quotation from a respected economist who points out very precisely where our troubles began.

The difficulty with a new start is to pinpoint the critical area where economics went astray... I would put it in the middle of the fourth chapter of Volume One of *The Wealth of Nations*... In (that) chapter, after discussing the need for

4 Alfred Eichner, *A Guide to Post-Keynsian Economics*, M. Sharpe, NY, 1979, vii.

money in a social economy, Smith suddenly gets fascinated by the distinction between money price, real money, and exchange value and from then on, hey presto, his interest gets bogged down in the question of how values and prices for products and factors are determined. One can trace a more or less continuous development of price theory from the subsequent chapters of Smith through Ricardo, Walras, Marshall, right up to Debreu and the most sophisticated present-day Americans.[5]

What are we looking for? We are seeking a realistic dynamic view that will hold to the concrete facts and possibilities of economic purpose and progress, that will not slip down the blind alley of general price analysis, that does not regard profits, losses, and interest rates as "the traffic lights of a free enterprise economy."[6] In terms of our automobile parallel, we are looking for an analysis of engine, drive-shaft, gears and wheels, that will dictate rhythms of driving no matter who drives, no matter what size the car is. In the Epilogue I will discuss how such a concrete realism will require, in its fullness, a massive cultural shift mediated by the end of what is presently known as philosophy. But meantime, in the text, we will focus on this lesser crossing of the Rubicon. "By the phrase, 'crossing the Rubicon', I mean this: however important those occasional excursions into sequence analysis may have been, they left the main body of economic theory on the 'static' bank of the river; the thing to do is not to supplement static theory by the booty brought back from these excursions but to replace it by a system of general economic dynamics into which statics would enter as a special case."[7]

5 Nicholas Kaldor, "The Irrelevance of Equilibrium Economics", *Economic Journal* (82) 1972, 1240-41.
6 Paul Krugman, *Peddling Prosperity*, Norton, N.Y., 1994, 36.
7 Joseph Schumpeter, *History of Economic Analysis*, Oxford University Press, 1954, 1160.

Since Keynes is associated popularly with a revolution in twentieth century economics, you may be puzzled at his absence in the text. The previous quotation is from Joseph Schumpeter, and I am not alone in regarding him as the more significant economist.[8] When Keynes does come close to our central topic, the treatment is pretty shabby.[9] Besides, Michael Kalecki would seem to have been better at doing what Keynes did.[10] But these are not beginners' topics. Nor, I would add, are my footnotes here or throughout the book: they point beyond the text in ways that will, I hope, be helpful to economists and to those interested in following up the larger challenge.

There is a bow to Marx, of course, in my subtitle: that subtitle will occupy us mainly in the Epilogue. At this stage it is best taken as a reading, Joyce-wise and with a Dublin accent, of the exclamation, "That's just capital!"[11] The view of economic realities towards which I point my reader is entirely derivative. I am merely trying to make available the achievement of Bernard Lonergan. He spent decades of his life struggling with the problem and in his final years wrote

8 Succinctly, Peter Drucker, "Schumpeter and Keynes", *Forbes*, May 23, 1982, 300-304; Robert Heilbroner, "Was Schumpeter Right After All?", *Journal of Economic Perspectives*, 7, 1993, 87-96. In the past decade there has been a new focus on Schumpeter with studies, biographies, conferences.

9 See *The General Theory of Employment, Interest and Money*, chapter 22: "Notes on the Trade Cycle".

10 Kalecki's essays of the early thirties anticipated Keynes' work and showed a broader perspective. See M. Kalecki, *Selected Essays on the Dynamics of the Capitalist Economy*, Cambridge University Press, 1972. See also note 11 of chapter 4.

11 The common meaning of *ius* has its root in the Sanskrit word, *yoh*, 'health'. A precise Christian meaning is discussed by Lonergan in *The Incarnate Word, Collected Works* Vol 8, University of Toronto Press, 1999, theses 15-17.

of *A Primer in Macroeconomic Dynamics* as a suitable title for his unfinished work.[12] I would like to think that the present little book prepares the way for such a primer.[13] So: let us begin.

12 A letter from Lonergan to Jane Collier, Cambridge University, June 12, 1982. (Lonergan Research Institute Archives, Toronto). I cannot exaggerate my dependence on Lonergan and his work. Scattered references throughout indicate facets of that dependence, going back to 1968 in economics, further still in methodologies to 1957. Two volumes of his economic writings will appear in 1999, as part of his *Collected Works*, being published by University of Toronto Press. Volume 15, edited by Patrick Byrne, Charles Hefling Jr. and Frederick Lawrence, deals with Lonergan's late efforts (1978-83) at presenting his views: it includes a substantial contextualizing introduction by Lawrence. Volume 21, edited by Philip McShane, contains Lonergan's original versions of the analysis, produced in 1942-44 after more than a decade of work. See further note 16 of the Epilogue. I shall refer to these volumes as *CWL* 15 and *CWL* 21 henceforth. Since the works are not yet available in final form, the references will be by section, or to the index.

13 In the Epilogue I shall return to the question of introducing, teaching, etc. It should become fairly evident to my reader, as he or she works along, that this is not a comprehensive indication of a proposed solution to our economic ills, not then of the character of Keynes' *General Theory*. It has its parallel in my experience of teaching introductory mathematical physics, opening up the students through imaginative exercises to later undergraduate and graduate courses. The cultural difficulty, of course, is that neither the thinking nor the texts of these later courses exist at present.

Baskets & Handfills

"It is time to go back to the beginning and start again."[1] The quotation is from a somewhat unorthodox introduction to economics that appeared and disappeared in the early seventies. It occurs at the end of a brief but illuminating survey of past economic theorizing, and is followed by the fresh beginning. One of the authors, Joan Robinson (1903-1983) was well-known for her disagreement with standard economics, especially American economics. Her little book, *Economic Heresies*, reaches back to her discussions with Keynes. At one point in that book she remarks that "Keynes' ideas were not always definite, precise and consistent,"[2] and recalls writing to Keynes about her difficulties in following the argument of chapter seventeen of *The General Theory*. "Keynes replied, in effect, that he was not surprised for he found it difficult himself."

You are not dismayed, I hope, by my mention of past economic theory and its difficulties, difficulties that are regularly glossed over in standard introductory texts. I am not going to plunge you into those murky waters. Indeed, if you have already suffered your way through an introductory course in economics, you will most

1 Joan Robinson and John Eatwell, *An Introduction To Modern Economics*, McGraw Hill, London and New York, 1973, 52. This work will henceforth be referred to as Robinson & Eatwell.
2 Joan Robinson, *Economic Heresies. Some Old-fashioned Questions in Economic Theory*. Basic Books, NY, 1973, 80.

likely be glad to hear that this, now, is the first and last mention in my little book of that famous IS/LM graph that so dominates such texts.[3]

So I am reaching with you for a fresh beginning, and part of that fresh beginning may be the growth of a fresh attitude in you. I will be asking you to imagine and puzzle, not in the context of any economic view or terminology, but in an openness to what goes on, or might go on, in the economy. You may already have the beginnings of that attitude, especially if you have been untouched by present economic teaching – even if you passed an introductory university course. On the other hand, if you graduated in economics and went on to higher things, you may find my approach too strange, indeed, unacceptable.

In this first chapter I want to invite you to think through what might appear to be a very simple distinction, the distinction between buying a plough for a farm business and buying a 5 lb bag of potatoes for your own use. This will be the main focus of the first part of the chapter. In the second part of the chapter I return to the two texts already mentioned, that by Robinson & Eatwell, and that by Gordon. We will reflect on the fresh beginning offered by the first text, and seek further light by reflecting on the standard beginning as illustrated by Gordon. This should help all my readers. Those uncorrupted by present economic theory will be helped towards a better grasp of the basic points of the first part of the chapter by glimpsing the strange world of those other presentations. Those

3 Robert J. Gordon, *Macroeconomics. Sixth Edition.* Harper Collins, NY, 1993. The index shows the extent of the dominance of the IS/LM view. "The IS/LM model has no greater prospect of being a viable analytic vehicle for macroeconomics in the 1990s than the Ford Pinto has of being a sporty, reliable car for the 1990s. Because of its treatment of expectations, the IS/LM model, as traditionally constructed and currently used, is a hazardous base on which to build positive theories of business fluctuations and to undertake policy analysis." Robert G. King, "Will the New Keynesian Macroeconomics resurrect the IS/LM Model?" *The Journal of Economic Perspectives* 7 (1993), 68.

comfortably familiar with standard views may be helped, by the contrasting and comparison, to more sympathy with the present approach. The chapter concludes with some further comments on the problem of attitude, orientation, regarding the basket of mental goods towards which I point you. Some readers may well leap, at least at a first reading, from the presentation of the first part of the chapter to those concluding remarks and so on to chapter two. If the elements of Newtonian astronomy are satisfying, why plunge into something less satisfying, like Ptolemaic astronomy, however fascinating that approach might be or plausible in its reference.

Before we venture onto our mythic island, Atlantis, with its potatoes and its emergent plough culture, we can profitably pause in imagination with a very primitive fruit-gathering and grain-gathering culture. This imaginative pausing is very important: indeed, you may gradually come to appreciate it as central to the revitalization of education in the next century.[4] I personally delight in returning, and bringing my philosophy students to return, and now bringing you to return, in imagination and active curiosity, to the invention of the wheel. I envisage an old pipe-smoking lady, as my grandmother was, sitting watching the moving of a large stone through the use of logs placed under it in sequence: in at the front, out behind, as the stone moves forward. The old lady comes up with the grand idea: *stop the middle*. It is the first step to the primitive cart. The gathering of fruit and grain are transformed.

So we can move back in mindful imagination to an earlier transformation, for prior to the cart there was the container, the

---

4 This is a topic to which I return regularly. The strategies in the text gently intimate a transformation of teaching, but the problem calls for deep fantasy. "If there is to be a massive shift in public minding and kindliness and discourse in the next century, there must be a proportionate shift in the mind and heart of the academy and the arts at the end of this century, with consequent changes in operating schemes of recurrence from government to kindergarten." P. McShane, *Lonergan's Challenge to the University and the Economy*, University Press of America, 1980, 1; Axial Press, second edition, forthcoming.

basket. You can envisage, now, a gathering of fruit or grain by hand-ful. It is brought by our small primitive group to a central spot, for storage is involved in their survival. The acute reader will realize that we are way back before cooking vessels and fire, or even drink-ing vessels. At all events, some bright person connects a broken coconut or shell with the possibility of a larger handful. The living of our little group is transformed.

I am talking here of changes in house or village management, innovations in the *oikonomos*.[5] Joseph Schumpeter, a great historian of economic theory, writes of such innovations using the notion "of Horizon. This we define as that range of choices within which a businessman moves freely and within which his decision for a course of action can be described."[6] The old lady's grand idea rep-resents a horizon-shift. The range of choices and courses of actions that blossom from it slowly, over centuries, involve further horizon-shifts: our group is a long way from the millwheel, the spinning jenny, the propeller. But you can envisage relatively immediate im-plementations of the idea, changing choices and courses of action in the small community, though you may find it hard to view the old lady as a business woman, furtively reaching the patent office to stake her claim!

It is as well, then, before we consider details of such transfor-mations, to add the more contemporary plough-illustration: I do not wish to strain your imagination by talking about the business of a legally-structured exchange economy among the fruit gatherers.

So we come to an enjoyment of the invention of the plough. I am not, of course, trying to plunge you into an interest in the history of agriculture, but I am trying to cultivate in you an attitude

---

5 The word reminds us of the early Greek reflections on the topic: *oikos* = home, *nomos* = law, measure. The book attempts to enlarge your sense of this word. In chapter 5 we will glimpse how we on the home-globe might reach the fullest humble measure of provision for the home-plate.
6 Joseph Schumpeter, *Business Cycles*, McGraw-Hill, New York, 1939, Vol 1, 99.

of concreteness, of realism, that will be important right through our efforts here and in future economic thinking. You may know nothing about the simple plough of early India, without wheel or moldboard – familiar to my Canadian readers as the angled plate at the front of a snowplough – or about the Chinese contribution of a padded horse-collar, or about the wheeled plough of 10th century Europe, but you can envisage concretely some achievement of turning the soil by a horse-pulled *tilted spade*. If you can do that, then you can enter into both our island story and into our reorientation of economic thinking.

We might well have taken for our island Prince Edward Island, famous for its potatoes, or Ireland, at some early part of an imagined history. But let us settle for the very small isolated island of Atlantis where, as our story begins, there is cultivation of the soil by spade, as well as village leisure in horse-racing, island transport by horse-cart, but no plough. Still, there is a tavern in the town, and the story opens therein with a group round a table that includes a lady, named Joey for she is a central character, who owns the main horse-stable, the gent who runs the local primitive bank, and a potato-farmer. As you get the point of the story you can add in other suitable characters: the blacksmith, the owner of the leather store, etc.

After some intake of the popular intoxicant, made from potatoes of course, (in Ireland we call it poiteen. Sometimes we allow it to age up to 48 hours; how about that for turnover frequency!) the talk turns towards potato cultivation. Such is the popularity of the racetrack, gambling, manufacturing ornaments, weaving intricate clothes, brewing and consuming poiteen, etc., that the farmer has a problem finding good help. The upshot of the discussion and the ferment is that – *eureka* – the horseowner gets the grand idea that if the farmer's spade could somehow be angled behind a horse and pulled by a horse, it would upgrade and uppace the tilling. And, of course, it would be good for both their businesses.

Again, we have the seed of a horizon-shift and a transformation of a local economy. In this case we can more plausibly suggest an exchange economy of a modern type. But all three cases – the wheel, the basket, the plough – illustrate the basic distinction that we focus on in this chapter, and indeed in the next. It is the distinction between primary and secondary activity, which is prior to distinguishing variations or stages in such activities. The most obvious illustration of the distinction is the difference between the basket and the fruit: you can't eat baskets. Still, the baskets facilitate eating, and indeed leisured eating.

Let us get the significance of the distinction clearer. When baskets are made available within our primitive group, fruit-gathering is no longer by the handful but by the basketful. Furthermore, the one basket can obviously be used indefinitely for gathering a basketful of fruit. Next we may add to this a division of suppliers. The horizon-shift gives rise to two groups of suppliers in the community: the suppliers of baskets and the suppliers of fruit, even if the latter are just self-suppliers. This is worth thinking out in concrete illustrations. One may take suppliers to be identically heads of families: the whole family is involved, say, in gathering, washing, weighing the fruit, but only the head of the family does the supplying, by means of some sort of selling. There may be one family in twenty whose occupation is with baskets. So you can certainly envisage two families, family F and family B, whose activities are respectively primary and secondary. There is the primary activity of supplying fruit; there is the secondary activity of supplying baskets as means of supplying fruit. If you take time here, you may move to the notion of tertiary and higher activities: the idea, for instance, of a certain type of needle for basket-weaving may add such levels. So, in a modern economy, you can identify machines or tools for making tools to make machines for secondary activities.

I must note here that such time-taking, such identification, is worthwhile, vital. Obviously, they are worthwhile as exercises in wit and imagination, exercises of the core of your humanity.[7] But they are worthwhile here in a necessary sense: without such pausing, such effortless effort, your agreement may well only be notional, nominal. You become a nodding acquaintance of the economic thinker, the semblance of an economist: you may even become a professor. Am I bordering on the ridiculous here, or labouring the obvious? In my long years in the academy, I saw too many students reach mindless masterly control over material, even move into the thin air of graduate studies. Robinson expresses the problem somewhat harshly with regard to economics:

> The student of economic theory is taught to write $O = f (L, C)$ where L is a quantity of labor, C a quantity of capital and O a rate of output of commodities. He is instructed to assume all workers alike, and to measure L in man-hours of labor; he is told something about the index number problem involved in choosing a unit of output; and then he is hurried on to the next question, in the hope that he will forget to ask in what units C is measured. Before ever he does ask, he has become a professor, and so sloppy habits of thought are handed on from one generation to the next.[8]

We will come to the thorny problem of measuring only in

7 Another angle on the problem indicated in note 4, above. Simply put, desire, curiosity, quest, are the core of your humanity. In my days of teaching philosophy I used give the beginning students a simple exercise. Go to the bookstore and check the indices of books on psychology, education, children, critical thinking, etc., for entries on *Questions*. Sometimes, under *Q*, they found *questionnaire*: but often there was no entry between *pubic hair* and *rats*. An unsettling illustration of our academic truncation: see notes 42, 43, 44, of chapter 5, and the text there.
8 Joan Robinson, "The Production Function in the Theory of Capital", *Review of Economic Studies* 21 (1955), 81.

chapter five. Our present problem is pace, beginner's pace. Perhaps an appeal to my own beginner's experience, at the age of forty, may help. Coming to grips with the nature and significance of the distinction that dominates this and the following chapter was a struggle not of months but of years.

Within the context of these odd asides perhaps you may begin to read better, more patiently, the economic process. As the French philosopher, Gaston Bachelard, was accustomed to say, you only begin to read seriously when you take your eyes off the page.[9] Does the idea of a tool for basket-making really add the possibility of a third and fourth level of activity? In what sense is the computer a modern tool for making tools for making tools? Are we caught here in some impossibly open hierarchy of levels of activity? Are we making unrealistic separations? Needles and computers seem very evidently to be components of primary activities. It takes not a little patient imagination to sort out such problems, to find that products, or even raw material, can fulfil functions on different levels, to figure out how higher layers of activities are actually interlaced.

Let me now introduce a simplifying grouping of activities. First, I call all activities that are primary, that provide immediately or mediately – think of leather on its way to being a shoe – consumables in the normal sense, basic activities. Consumables in the normal sense are goods and services that go into the standard of living. In a less normal sense, basic activities consume the goods and services of the other levels of activity. Secondly, it is convenient to consider all the other levels of activity as one group, as activities of the surplus level. I was tempted to name this group simply the plus level, avoiding thus both a Marxist distraction and an etymological curiosity, but the terminology is Lonergan's and there seems no inconvenience in sticking with it. Should we stick to the terminology and its implied division permanently? The terminology

9 See Gaston Bachelard, *The Poetics of Space*, Beacon Press, Boston, 1970, pages 14, 21, 39, 47, 83 on the challenge of reading adequately.

reaches far before Marx, and the division is relatively permanent in its significance for the understanding and measurement of rhythms of production. One may, of course, suspect a later millennium when a higher level idea would call for refinements in theory, production, financing, measurement. But the distinction between basic and non-basic activities is a permanent feature of future economic analysis.

So, two levels of economic activity are distinguished: a basic level and a surplus level. The basic level is the provider of what are normally recognized as consumer goods and services. The basic level is also consumer to the surplus level; the surplus level is consumer to itself. I am using the word *consumer* here but curiously I am not talking about anybody: I am talking about a level of activity of anybody. Again, I must ask you to ponder over this until you sense that you have it reasonably straight. I invite you, indeed, to ponder and wander, to check your neighbourhood and your cash. In my own village of Riverside, New Brunswick, we have two stores where I make purchases of bread and butter, spades and stamps, petrol and paint. In both stores I rent videos. While we have yet to detail varieties of financial transactions, we can still profitably ask about my local transactions and yours, and local transactions of others, in relation to our initial description, or more properly, explanation.

My transactions would seem to be simple: am I not just a basic consumer? And are not the activities of the two sets of shopkeepers likewise easily identified? The trouble is that we are struggling towards functional, explanatory, distinctions. Certainly, most of my purchases are basic: but what of the purchases of stamps for correspondence with a publisher? What of the purchases of petrol when the purchase is for my wife's car, with a business (Is the United Church of Canada a business?!) allowance for such purchases? The video rental is even more complex, as is renting generally: and think of the problem of renting money! At all events, one must note that an activity is identifiable by its economic function. Truckers buy gas and farmers buy spades at one of the local stores: are both these types of activity surplus activities? Even the bread and butter are not safe: does the trucker have a lunch allowance? Throw in the question of immediate purchase taxes – in Canada we have a double tax, provincial and federal, one feeding off the other. Only later will we be able to specify the indirect manner in which that portion of my seemingly innocent spending functions. Then, of course, there is the old age pension which makes some of my purchases possible: what sort of activity gets my monthly cheque to me?

But sorting all these out in a way that will be of scientific and practical significance is the task of the next few chapters. It is sufficient for now to note a complexity calling for an effort of understanding that goes beyond facile description in economics and the models based on it: landlords and peasants, capitalists and labourers, land and corn. An analogy may help here. Millennia of alchemy and descriptive chemistry preceded the breakthroughs of Mendeleev and Meyer in the 1860s. There is nothing obvious about the relational structuring of elements that these two men brought into scientific being. Nor was there a rush to accept it: but now the periodic table is part of our culture. That shift in chemistry stands out as the major paradigm shift in the field. Is something similar possible in economics? Certainly something similar seems necessary: Joan Robinson is not alone in her view of the deficiencies of present economic theory, of the need for a new beginning. And it would help us on our way to pause over her own struggle, with John Eatwell, towards a freshening of economic theory. But first we should gather the key directions in our own searchings.

We are trying to identify, in a preliminary fashion, two types of flow in economic process: a basic flow of activities and a surplus flow of activities. It is not too difficult to envisage a steady state of such activities: there is the provision of spades, there is the provision of potatoes. If our isolated island has a fairly stable population with fairly stable habits, then the two flows vary little, and the spade business is primarily a replacement business. Next, we turn our attention to innovation seeded by an idea. There are, of course, other types of innovation due to changes of habits of industry, procreation, religion, entertainment, that represent shifts that are not radically insightful. Economists could talk here, for instance, of a *widening of capital.* But we are interested here in significant horizon-shifts: the discovery of basket or plough, railway or computer.

Let us stay with our island of Atlantis and its tavern-discovery of the possibility of horse-digging. Someone with literary talent could fill a substantial amount of paper to stimulate our imagination and understanding of the shifting of daily life on the island. Here I must leave that to the talent of my reader. We already noted the involvement of a primitive bank, but we are not asking whether, or how, activities of the bank fit into either flow. That will concern us in chapter three. What is important to notice is a rhythm to the island's change. One can imagine a certain sub-group of the population, backed by our friendly banker, getting the project going. The sub-group is not isolated: there would be a general initial lift to the island's activities. But notice some lags. The plough culture, like Rome, is not built in a day. There is the breeding, training and outfitting of horses, while new ways of smithing, carpentry, leather working, emerge. Will it all take a season or even a year or three?[10] And meantime, even if basic activities have felt the lift, there has not been a new abundance of potatoes or potato derivatives such as poiteen. There is then, an expansion of surplus activities but only after a lag, perhaps a considerable lag, is there an input from this expansion into an expansion of basic activities that leads to a shift in the bulk and character of consumer supplies. Moreover, the expansion of basic activities, providing new varieties of potato-soup and new rhythms of alcohol consumption, coincides with a leveling off of the surplus expansion. Notice that I speak of a leveling off,

10 The problem, of course, is an empirical one. Three year cycles are associated with the names of two economists, Kitchin and Crum. See notes 16, 17, 18 of chapter 5.

not of a slump. I am envisaging, of course, a pretty bright pre-medieval people who foresee, and are content with, the shift to replacement and maintenance business. You can surely conceive of other scenarios, for we are surrounded by them. The plough-makers can seek out another island to keep business going, or generate a fashion of replacing ploughs annually through persuasion or built-in obsolescence or micro-improvements. But these scenarios raise other topics. At this stage we are content to notice, as concretely as your leisured imagination permits, certain rhythms of expansion that eventually give rise to a new dynamic steadiness of economic activities. This is not, of course, the whole story. Your leisured imagination, or your familiarity with history, will conjure up for you problems of people and businesses stuck in their ways, digging in to a past without ploughs, or simply holding on till a bitter end. Joseph Schumpeter, to whom I refer regularly, prior to his career as an economist in America, was finance minister of Austria during the appalling inflation there of 1922: at the end of that year the crown was down to 70,000 to the dollar compared to 4.9 to the dollar before the Great War. The lesson seems to have left him with the view that bankruptcy and its concomitants were part of the economic scene, in need of analysis. Whatever the unnaturalness of those events, it is wise to keep such sub-processes in mind in the search for an understanding of economic surges.

By way of contrast with our type of seeking we now turn to the text with which we began this chapter, *An Introduction to Modern Economics*. I pick this text, not because of its deficiencies, on which I mainly focus, but because I regard it as a magnificent but failed effort to reach a new basis of economic analysis. If the text is available to you, all the better, but that is not essential to our effort. I will sketch sufficiently the direction that Robinson & Eatwell take so as to lead us forward to a helpful contrast. The quotation at the beginning of this chapter comes from the conclusion of Book One of the text, which provides an enlightening summary of economic theorizing in these past centuries. Our concern here is with the next section, Robinson and Eatwell's fresh start, which involves introductory comments on method followed by a chapter on 'Land and Labour'. The second chapter, 'Men and Machines', will be drawn on midway through chapter three, below, to throw light on our own efforts to account for basic and surplus activities and the flows of payments that they involve.

We turn, then, to some reflections on the new beginning for economic analysis in *An Introduction to Economic Analysis*. You will, I hope, immediately notice a difference from our approach, a difference that you will come gradually to appreciate as a deeply-destructive disorientation. Our orientation so far has been a clinging to the concrete, a searching attention to the mess and mesh of the flux of economic history, in order to let it, so to speak, jar us into a discovery of the relevant economic variables. It is the method of serious science, whether in physics or in history.[11] Robinson & Eatwell, on the other hand, take their cue from Ricardo: "Far more than Quesnay, he deserves the title of the father of modern economics, for he devised the method of analysis which we know as setting up a model. The method consists of extracting the bare essentials of a problem, cutting out all irrelevant details, and examining the interactions between its parts."[12] They enlarge on this strategy in the first page of the new beginning.

> The method is to select from the flux of history (including the present as history) entities such as commodities, prices, monetary units, cultivable land, productive equipment,

11 Again, a large topic, and a deep present problem related to the problems pointed to in notes 4 and 7 above. On the method of physics, see B. Lonergan, *Insight*, Longmans, Green and Co., 1957; *Collected Works*, volume 3, University of Toronto Press, 1992, chapters 1-5. On the method of history, see B. Lonergan, *Method in Theology*, Herder and Herder, New York, 1972, chapters 8 and 9.
12 Robinson & Eatwell, 11.

employers, workers, and owners of wealth, specify the economic environment in which they are to interact, and set
them up in a model in which their interactions are worked
out by a quasi-mathematical logic.[13]

Apart altogether from the muddle about models in science,
we may note the more elementary problem that lurks behind the
word *select*, or the earlier word *extracting*. It took many centuries for
Newton to select the essentials from the flux of astronomical history and the centuries of puzzling about it. Meyer's & Mendeleev's
extracting the bare essentials of chemical relations came after millennia
of alchemy and chemistry and called for an open focus on the flux
of both chemical phenomena and theorizing about it. The selecting
and extracting that lifts inquiry to a level of serious understanding
is a cruxifyingly creative surge from the phenomenal flux to terms
and relations that seem utterly remote from push and pull, fire and
weight, and, in our case, from "commodities, prices, monetary units,
cultivable land, productive equipment, employers, workers, and
owners of wealth". The fresh start called for by Robinson, or more
generally by the post-Keynesians,[14] requires a massive creative shift
of focus. "Economics has to rely on the experiments thrown up by
events"[15]: this certainly is true. But without a hard-won grasp of the
fundamental events, the experiments of history can be swept into a
cloudy discourse about mercantilism and communism, greenbacks
and assignats, workers and capitalists, marginal products and Phillips'
curves, natural rates of unemployment, profit, growth, etc. What I
have been pointing you towards is a reach for the hard-won grasp
of the aggregates of events that are distinguishable and significant
economic flows.

13 *Ibid*, 53.
14 See note 4 of the Prologue. Both Robinson and Eichner had a hand in found-
ing *The Journal of Post-Keynesian Economics*.
15 Robinson & Eatwell, 54.

It is too early in our effort to go beyond these general pointers in any detail. A separate essay, or indeed a book, would be required to treat these few pages of Robinson and Eatwell adequately and to place them into the context of debates regarding the methodology of economics.[16] So, I restrict my comments here to some few directives in Robinson and Eatwell that help towards glimpsing what we will be attempting in the following chapters.

The first directive to note is an insistence that has muddied economic thinking since its beginnings: "The most essential element to include in any piece of analysis is an indication of the nature of the social system to which it is applied."[17] The drive of our analysis is away from this distraction towards fundamental functional distinctions. In so departing from conventional economics we eventually arrive at a perspective on distribution and justice that out-marks Marx.

The second directive continues the model business. It is worth quoting fully.

> The method of analysis is to skin off all the details and expose the mechanism of the system in a simplified form. In what follows we pursue this method in an extremely drastic manner. For instance, in the first three chapters we rule out all problems of relative prices and patterns of demand by working with a model in which there is only a single, uniform consumable good. When we are discussing agriculture, we abstract from variations in the weather. We assume that all workers are alike, and abstract from the dif-

16 Another large problem zone, tying in with those commented on above, note 11. A handy introduction to the area is M. Blaug, *The Methodology of Economics*, Cambridge, 1980, with an introductory chapter (pages 1 to 28) on "What you always wanted to know about the philosophy of science but were afraid to ask." Blaug shares the contemporary truncation, but there are much worse texts.
17 Robinson & Eatwell, 54.

ferences between men and women. The object of the exercise is to display relationships that are important in reality, though in reality they are overlaid with intricate complications. Before any conclusion from such an argument can be applied to reality, the relevant details have to be put back.[18]

The third and last directive to be considered brings together the previous two to give the fresh start to economic analysis. "We first consider an economy consisting of independent peasant families living on a wide, uniformly fertile plain."[19] A wide, uniformly fertile plain does not seem far from our island. Yet the pages to follow in *An Introduction to Modern Economics* bear little resemblance to our struggle with flows, with their distinction, with the effect of innovation on them. There is, of course, no tavern in the plain: changing the unique product, corn, to corn-mash, would be an inadmissible creative shake-up to the model.

Still, the authors manage to move quickly from considerations of a stationary state to problems of growth, diminishing returns, overhead labour, landlords and peasants, moneylenders. Furthermore, all the standard problems concerning capital, profit, wages, crowd in. A cluster of diagrams follow, on land, labour, incomes, output, marginality, etc., before the reader finally gets some pointers on the mess of neoclassical economics.

All in all, I suspect that you will sense, even without that text to hand, that our first chapter is neater, cleaner. But do not be deceived: the problems are all there, even in our stationary state, the island of potato-diggers, especially if there are moneylenders on the island. The problems become more acute when major innovations occur, especially if the mentality is such that, as Robinson and

18 *Ibid*, 55.
19 *Ibid*, 64.

Eatwell describe Richardo's scheme, "it is natural for a capitalist to be ambitious and to want to expand his operations to increase the flow of his profits."[20] A certain malice or madness is, then, assumed by these authors to be natural in the plough-making business as some would suspect it is now in the car-making business.

Our initial effort leaves none of this out. I have not attempted to "skin off all the details and expose the mechanism of the system in a simplified form."[21] Rather, I have invited you to discover in the details essential features of the mechanism of the system. Or rather, to move into an attitude of discovery that will carry you through the distracting details towards a focus on the key flows of the economic mechanism.

In chapter three we will return to the text to bring out features of the achievements of Robinson & Eatwell in their sorting out of a simple economy that produces both a consumer good and new machines for that production. The new machines need not be really *new*, like our ploughs, but you will be able to recognize our distinction of the two flows, and appreciate from their model the need for our concrete heuristics of production and finance.

We might well conclude our introductory searching here, but it may be worthwhile for some – depending on your background – to pause over the standard text-book introduction to economics, from which Robinson & Eatwell wish to rescue us. If this does not interest you, either because you have already been disillusioned by some introductory text or because such texts are quite foreign to you, then you may wish to go directly to chapter two, or to my concluding comments in this chapter.

The standard text that I wish to use is one that I have already mentioned when referring to that henceforth unmentionable graph. But any standard text in macroeconomics will suffice. The first edition of Gordon's book happens to be a text that Bernard Lonergan

20 *Ibid*, 76.
21 *Ibid*, 55.

used in his presentation of his *Essay in Circulation Analysis* in Boston College Theology Department around the early eighties. It was not that the text showed any agreement with Lonergan's view, but that it was a lucid account of the standard view. The text I use, the sixth edition, is a much improved update, placing the post-1973 American slowdown in an international context, with some focus on business cycles. Nonetheless, any text will do if you wish to peruse standard teaching, and no text is required. The main focus of my attention, indeed, will be two common diagrams of the circulation of products and money, which I will reproduce immediately.[22]

A SIMPLE IMAGINARY ECONOMY

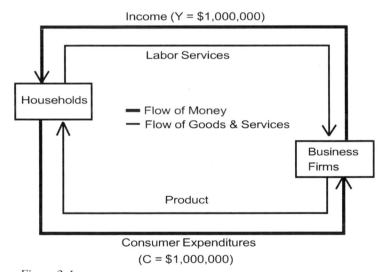

Figure 2-1
The Circular Flow of
Income and Consumer Expenditures
The circular flow of income and expenditure in a simple imaginary economy in which households consume their entire income. There aare no taxes, no government spending, no saving, no investment, and no foreign sector.

22 The diagrams are from pages 29 and 35 of the text cited above, note 3.

SAVING LEAKS OUT OF THE SPENDING STREAM BUT
REAPPEARS AS INVESTMENT

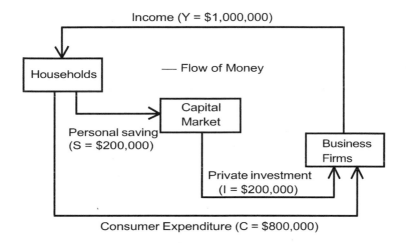

Income (Y = $1,000,000)

Households — Flow of Money

Capital
Market

Personal saving
(S = $200,000)

Business
Firms

Private investment
(I = $200,000)

Consumer Expenditure (C = $800,000)

Figure 2-3
Introduction of Saving and
Investment to the Circular Flow Diagram
Our simple imaginary economy (Figure 2-1) when households
save 20 percent of their income. Business firms' investment
accounts for 20 percent of total expenditure. Again, we are
assuming that there are no taxes, no government spending, and
no foreign sector.

The first diagram is of a very simple economy in which households consume their entire income: there are no taxes, no government
spending, no saving, no investment, and no foreign sector. Gordon,
in fact, does give a third diagram that includes these later in this
chapter, but it is too early in our struggle to face such complications,
and at all events the point I wish to make springs easily from the
first two diagrams. The second diagram adds household savings,
which in this simple economy flow through the capital market to
become investments. This makes evident that famous relationship,
savings equal investments, which of course is not true, but we will
get to that later.

What I wish you to take note of and ponder over with regard to the two diagrams is that our distinction between types of products, basic and surplus, is absent. It would be an interesting exercise for you to try to amend, say, the first diagram to include that distinction. There is a line from Business Firms to Households titled 'Product'. From a beginner's grasp of our distinction you might suspect that two lines are needed, the second line beginning and ending at the Business Firms. But then you need to add another income line. Nor will this be satisfactory. Don't wear yourself out: pass on to some similar puttering with the second diagram. Here we simply have a money flow, the topic of our third chapter: one must assume that products somehow flow the other way, yet obviously without passing through Wall Street or its equivalent. You will find it illuminating to come back to this diagram after working through our chapter three. But even now, does your beginner's glimpse already give you a suspicion that there are missing flows that are essential to our understanding even of this elementary economy? The key word here is *essential*, raising the interlocking questions, what is essential, the essence and how does one come to the essential?

Let us consider the first question: in its fullness it is, of course, the question of the essence of economics, on which much ink has been spilled. Here I wish only to pursue the question in regard to the distinction between basic and surplus production. The implicit claim of our introductory chapter is that it is of the essence of both stable or progressive economies. The further claim, here and in chapter two, is that it is not easy to reach and to appreciate. The distinction lifts you beyond households and firms, houses and factories, to the challenge of understanding economic process in terms of explanatory functions. You will find, or have already found, that no amount of juggling will get the two diagrams into a worthwhile perspective because the diagrams trap the reader in non-functional description. Such entrapment is a cousin to the way in which Robinson & Eatwell are trapped by social arrangements. We will find, however, when we reach the end of chapter three, that Robinson & Eatwell do have elements of analysis that break towards our functional distinctions. Not so Gordon. He shares the common view that "theory throws a spotlight on just a few key relations,"[23] "theory isolates the important economic variables,"[24] but the relations and variables that are the focus of our attention find no place in his analysis. This fact, which is a reality of most elementary economics courses, should help to sharpen the question raised in the present chapter and followed through in the entire book: Are the variables, basic and surplus production, and their relations, someway of the essence both of economic behaviour and of economic analysis?

We turn now to the second question: how does one arrive at a grasp of the essential? Here, I'm afraid, we are touching on a massive philosophical and educational disorientation. A few hints must suffice.[25]

I have been inviting you, and will continue so to invite, to enter into our search imaginatively, with leisured curiosity and patient illustration. I do this in agreement with Aristotle and Thomas Aquinas regarding how your mind and my mind work. Robinson and Eatwell attempted something similar without serious methodological advertence: it was a basis of some criticism of their efforts.[26] Gordon, on the other hand, follows a comfortable conventional mindlessness, summed up in his introductory claims: "By the middle of Chapter 3, all students will have learned the concepts essential to understanding the new material to be developed"[27]; "The basic

23 *op. cit.*, notes 3, 5.
24 *Ibid.*, 22.
25 The key effort of retrieval here is B. Lonergan, *Word and Idea in Aquinas*, University of Notre Dame Press, 1967; *Collected Works*, volume 2, University of Toronto Press, 1996. In it he rescues the meaning, for Aristotle and for Aquinas, of *essence* and of its slow discovery.
26 Marjorie Turner, *Joan Robinson and the Americans*, M.E. Sharpe, Armour, N.Y., 1990, 175-9, gives an account of the reception of the Robinson & Eatwell book.
27 Gordon, op. cit., note 4, xxv.

task of macroeconomics is to study the behavior of each of the six concepts" that he introduces in the first chapter.[28] What does Gordon mean by 'concept' here? I would suggest that he means a name to which familiarity and memorization add detailed referents during the student's struggle. The struggle does not leave permanent results, unless the student continues circling the *concepts* in upper courses that can blossom into graduate studies, even into the stale comfort of professorial familiarity. The phenomenon is not restricted to economics. At the beginning of each academic year I found it enlightening, as did my students in philosophy, to discuss their reaction to being asked to repeat the exams they had done in the early summer. You may guess the answer.

What, then, do I mean by a concept, a serious explanatory concept, such as we struggle towards in these chapters? I can perhaps appeal to the description that I regularly, in the past twenty years, invited my students of philosophy to ponder over. There are two characteristics of a serious explanatory concept. You will remember the weeks, months, even years, that you spent – with feats of curiosity, not feats of memory – in struggling towards it. You will be able, even years later, to speak of it coherently, illuminatingly, through illustrations, for perhaps ten hours. Maybe you are led by this to suspect that serious explanatory concepts are rare achievements? And certainly they are not passed on from generation to generation in compact little learned nuggets.

Consider, for example, the serious explanatory concept of money. Galbraith, in his entertaining little book titled *Money, Whence it Came, Where it Went*, remarks at the beginning, "There is nothing about money that cannot be understood by the person of reasonable curiosity, diligence and intelligence. There is nothing on the following pages that cannot be so understood."[29] This, surely, I must agree with, even while quibbling about the suggested fullness of

28 *Ibid.*, 2.
29 JK Galbraith, *Money, Whence it Came, Where it Went*, Penguin, Introduction.

understanding. I hope that you will agree, too, in relation to the following pages of this little book. Later, on the same page, Galbraith adds:

> Television interviewers with a reputation for penetrating thought regularly begin interviews with economists with the question: 'Now tell me, just what is money anyway?' The answers are invariably incoherent. Teachers of elementary economics or money and banking begin with definitions of genuine subtlety. These are then carefully transcribed, painfully memorized and mercifully forgotten. The reader should proceed in these pages in the knowledge that money is nothing more or less than what he or she always thought it was.

The reader who so proceeds with Galbraith's book will end up with an interesting perspective on the messy and erroneous manipulation of money in history, especially in America up to 1975. But no serious grasp of the nature, the essence, of money will be generated, for it is not on offer. A beginning of such a grasp is on offer here, especially in chapter three where an explanatory meaning of money is laced into the explanatory meaning of economic rhythms and surges.[30] My reader is invited to take a very different stance than

---

30 It is valuable to emphasize, at the end of this chapter, the point made at the conclusion of the Prologue, and to do so in a definite context. The book aims at a beginning. A new *Treatise On Money* must come later, springing from a dialectic retrieval of past and present struggles (see note 4 of the Epilogue). "If it is recognized that money may act as a disturber, then the problem arises of defining how money would have to behave in order to leave the real processes of the barter model uninfluenced. Wicksell was the first to see the problem clearly and to coin an appropriate concept, Neutral Money... an interesting case of a concept's rendering valuable service by proving unworkable" (Schumpeter, *History of Economic Analysis*, 1088-9). What is needed, for the dynamic model, is a heuristic concept of Enmeshed Money that will gradually, with rich consistency, cover issues associated with such topics as interest rates, monetary policy, credit facilitation, national and international debts, the earnings of stocks, bonds, banking, brokerage, etc., and the laws of rhythmic and diminishing returns on finance.

that which Galbraith suggests for his readers. It is the stance of a curious and patient expectation of unexpected horizon-shifts such as I mentioned at the beginning of the chapter. The nature of such shifting is a profoundly difficult topic, but your effort to so shift here will, I hope, make that topic topical, essential as it is to the cultural transformation required for genuine economic enlightenment.

Enough of these pointers. Perhaps I have led you to suspect that the essence of the standard basket of goods is as elusive as James Joyce's artistic essence of the basket,[31] that you have here a handfill as elusive as the spelling of water that handfilled Helen Keller for five uncomprehending weeks?[32] If so, you may find that the terror of transformation[33] has a wide variety of excusing disguises. But I do hope that you will still try the foothills, handholds, of chapter two.

---

31 James Joyce, *The Dubliners*, Penguin, 211-213.

32 Those events of 1887 in Helen's life, dealt with in various biographies, are eloquently captured in the film *The Miracleworker*. The topic of Helen's discovery of language is treated in McShane, *A Brief History of Tongue*, Axial Press, 1998, chapter one.

33 There is need for a transposition of metaphorical talk of transformations and neuroses, terror and monsters, into a heuristic explanatory perspective. Still, Jung makes the point plainly when he writes, "If a man is a hero, he is a hero because, in the first reckoning, he did not let the monster devour him, but subdued it not once but many times." "The Relations between the Ego and the Unconscious", *Collected Works*, volume 7, 173. See P. McShane, *Process*, Axial Press, forthcoming, chapters 3 and 4 for some introductory reflections on ontogenetic and phylogenetic transformations.

Flows & Surges

The problem now is to work our, your, way towards grasping significant variables of the productive process. The productive process to be considered, imaginatively puzzled over, will initially be your local productive process: by the end of the chapter the local will have become the global. Within some reasonable distance from you there is an urban instance of the complexities of the modern provision of goods and services. We are no longer, then, dealing with baskets and ploughs, fruit and potatoes. We are dealing with your local factories and stores, offices and banks, restaurant cooks and road-workers, television shows and bus stations, trucks and bicycles, prostitutes and pawnshops. Our thinking has to be very far from an old style economic theorizing in terms of corn and a mysterious capital substance. We are interested in holding to the concrete and identifying flows. We already made a start on this in chapter one, where we identified an elementary or basic flow and a distinct, more complex, surplus, flow. There was a basic flow of potatoes and berries and loaves, a certain number per time interval the variation of which we have not explicitly considered. There was a distinct flow of ploughs and baskets, again a certain number per time interval, starting obviously from zero at the time of their invention. Higher flows certainly occur, roughly identifiable as flows of machine tools, and we will occasionally explicitly identify these as definite levels of the surplus flow.

The present exercise involves extending our elementary identifications to the modern urban, national and international economy, though our focus remains the two flows in an isolated economy. These are the basic and surplus flows of activities that begin, carry forward, and end, the productive process. One must think of the productive process, then, as linking the potentialities of nature, including human nature, at its beginning, with the actual standard of living, where it ends. It is solely the current process that is involved. The bags of groceries carried from the store are no longer part of the process: they are part of the standard of living. What about the store? It was certainly once part of the process, but it no longer is: only its use is part of the process. Already here we are in surprisingly deep water: or, rather, we are preparing to avoid murky waters of measurement problems that we will deal with to some extent in chapter five. So, our elementary distinctions are worth more effort than you might expect at this stage. Briefly, then, what are commonly known as consumer goods pass out of the productive process to become elements in the standard of living; what are commonly known as producer goods, when completed, move into the process at a lower level, as means of production. A train under production is within the productive process; the finished, sold, train is not, but its use is.

The astute reader will have noticed my slipping in the word, *sold*. As yet I have avoided considerations of media of exchange, the topic of the next chapter, but what we envisage, of course, is an exchange economy. So, a good or service is completed, leaves the process, only when it is sold. We will return later to questions of waste, second-hand re-entry, etc.

We are thinking of two main flows of activities, and each flow involves planning and production and sales activities. These activities vary enormously according to technical and cultural developments, and by varying your own illustrative base you may come to grasp the fundamental character of the flows: a succession of both rhythmic and flexible activities beginning with the potentialities of nature and ending either in the standard of living – then they are activities of the basic flow – or in moving into use in the next lowest flow. I must leave to my reader the envisagement of such flows as, for example, the activities that lead from fields to flax to linen shirts, from mines to steel to linen mills. You would be well advised also to return to the list of the first paragraph of this chapter, even to enlarge on it, in order to discover more precisely both the breadth and the narrowness of our characterization of the two significant flows. You will note immediately that there are other flows: neither banks nor pawnshops nor brokers nor real estate agents seem to fit comfortably into what is being identified as the productive process. You may note also that such activities as prostitution, protection rackets, the stolen car business, various institutions of gambling, can easily be located in our flows: the problem with these is not classification but the problem of measuring the rates of underground economic activities.

Again, you may be startled to find how much of what you spontaneously consider to be wealth does not belong in our identification of significant goods. What, for instance, of suburbia? In so far as you have grasped that our interest is not in static wealth but in dynamic wealth, then you can distinguish between the vast static suburban reality and the potentialities and activities of its inhabitants. You can follow this up by trying to identify what activities of the inhabitants belong to either flow of the productive process. And what of the flow of activities that transports the inhabitants to the city centre? There are bus drivers, drivers of a company car, drivers in part or total ownership of the car that is being used. In the one and only time that I have ever presented this stuff verbally – in Boston College, 1977 – I invited my listeners to engage in the discomforting exercise of identifying functionally the flow of traffic on a Boston street. It is discomforting, because one finds how removed one is from a spontaneous competence of identification. Such a spontaneous competence, of course, is part of the remote project of economic education. "If a biologist takes his young son to the zoo and both pause to look at a giraffe, the boy will wonder whether it bites or kicks, but the father will see another manner in which skeletal, locomotive, digestive, vascular, and nervous systems combine and interlock."[1] Present economists, like the boy, may wonder – at times with vast mathematical complexity – how it buys or sells: we are pushing towards a significant scientific perspective on interlocking flows.

I am not trying here to confuse you with particulars: I am hoping rather that you will accept my invitation to maintain the leisured concrete reference that will bring you both the slow accumulation of little insights and also the growing sense that our shift, what we are tackling, is not easy. A parallel from the history of chemistry may help. Chemistry was bogged down, for centuries, by the obviousness of fire burning, and the obvious conclusion that there was such a reality as phlogiston. Lavoisier offered a discomforting shift from the obviously observed. I am inviting you to a like shift, from the obviousness of the edge of economic process – buying and selling, profit and *gross product* – to the functional heart of the process. Imagine it in any way that will help you towards insights: two flow pipes, one above the other. Can you figure out an imaginative connection? Certainly, it is not like connecting water pipes. Diagrams are necessary, and the struggle with deficient diagrams helps both towards better insight and better diagrams. So, we have something like two flow pipes. At the entry of each there are nature's and human nature's potentialities. At the end there are the flows of products out of the system, bought out of the system. The basic flow ends in consumer wealth and *socially-established* well-being: bread and honey, cars and houses. The first-order surplus flow ends by being bought into the basic flow, for its use there, in a raising of the potentialities of nature and human nature. Now, or later, you will notice that the simple 'in at one end, out at the other' does not really fit the reality. Why? I hope that, whether you are economically-learned or not, you are distracted here into difficulties and doubts about lags and inventories, over-production and ineffective

1 B. Lonergan, *Method in Theology*, Herder and Herder, New York, 1972, 82-3.

demand, and of course the issue of what may be considered at this stage as the *counterflows*, the issue of media of exchange. I can only plead for patience.

At this stage what I seek is primarily a sympathetical acknowledgement of the legitimacy of the distinction of the two flows, each involving aggregates of rates of activity, no measure of which has yet been introduced. Some may find it odd that I have made no mention either of ownership and property, of capitalists and workers, beyond the introduction of sales as a transition-place out of each flow of the process. Here again we are avoiding a zone of obviousness that distracts from our present focus, that has distracted economists for centuries into shabby analyses.

But I would have you yield to leisurely economic distractions as you pause in your own locale. I write now as I sit outdoors in the early morning light of September watching cattle on the Fundy marshes, savouring the way in which enlivened distractions can lead to an enriched perspective. It is Clara Schumann's birthday and her music has been on the airwaves. How odd, to think of Clara Schumann's music as part of the productive process. Does the broadcast differ, as part of the process, if the radio is not commercial? Is the provision of compact discs an activity of the basic flow? Is Clara connected with an improvement in the potentialities of nature? In what way is Clara's life and music still part of the process, permanently part of the standard of living?

Such cultivated distractions help us towards a sense of the difficulty of determining the nature and significance of the flow variables in current process. Especially there is the difficulty raised by asking the curious question, how long is current process? In terms of an earlier image, how long are those two flowpipes?

The question, put that way with one sense of *current*, is analogous to the problem of *current history*. My step-son returned home from school this week to inform me that his medieval history course began with early African hominids. Wow! As I look out over the

Fundy marshes I appreciate the ways in which they have been part of the current productive process for quite some time. From conception to beyond death the cattle on the marsh are part of current process. What, then, is the time-measure of current process? At my elbow this fine morning I happen to have JJ von Duijn's *The Long Wave in Economic Life.*[2] For him, as for Juglar and Marx and Schumpeter and Rostow, current process can be said to span centuries. Current process, then, is a matter of focus, but I would insist that it is necessarily a historical focus, bringing with it all the psychological and methodological problems laced into such a focus, and cutting away from such extremes as the Walrasian Now, or an economics of Kingdom Come.[3] And, of course, there are the other wonderlands of a modelling business based on assumptions acceptedly ahistorical, or of an economy of perfect competition. The latter wonderland helps bring up the problem of focus for the individual in business for herself or himself: the focus then is regularly tied into turnover frequencies and seasonal opportunities, and perfect competition means doing better than the next guy.[4]

What is our focus? The focus has been, perhaps, at least vaguely evident to you from the first page of chapter one: we are interested in the effect of major positive innovative changes on the dynamics of the productive process. The time-span of our focus will be dictated by that interest. The interest is a variable which may reach back to medieval farming or forward to the fourth millennium without changing attention from such a vista as the ridges of Port Meadow

---

2 JJ van Duijn, *The Long Wave in Economic Life*, Allen and Unwin, London, 1983.
3 Joan Robinson deals with both these topics in a reasonably popular fashion in *Economic Heresies*, Basic Books, New York, 1973.
4 "Is it not a fact that what we mean (by competitive business) is the scheme of motives, decisions, and actions imposed upon a business firm by the necessity of doing things better or at any rate more successfully than the fellow next door… ?" Schumpeter, *History of Economic Analysis,* 975.

in Oxford.[5] But this very looseness of the meaning of *current* helps me to bring the reader back to the tight meaning of *current* – *currens*, – flowing, that is the deeper systematic issue. Whether we home in on the early economy of China or on the economic potential of Antarctica, we focus on flows.

There are various other possible confusions about interest in the dynamics of the productive process which we had best sort out at this early stage in our struggle. One of our initial illustrations of economic process in change involved the transition from a digging culture to a plough culture. Both the settled cultures and the transitional stage are obviously dynamic. The transitional stage can conveniently be called an evolutionary state; the settled stage of either the digging culture or the fully-operative plough culture can be called a stationary state.[6] All three stages are dynamic, and investigating that dynamic is the heart of our project, our analysis, our dynamic analysis in that sense, though I prefer to speak simply of analysis. A further appeal to Schumpeter may help the reader along here. "Let us recall once more that here, as throughout the book, Dynamics means exclusively analysis that links quantities pertaining to different points of theoretic time – in the sense that has been repeatedly explained before – and not the theory of evolutionary processes that run their courses in historic time."[7] Schumpeter goes on to speak of Marshall as failing to cross the Rubicon, and it is worth repeating his characterization of that crossing.

5 See P. McShane, *Randomness, Statistics and Emergence*, Gill and Macmillan, Dublin, 1970, 72-76, for reflections on the investigation of Port Meadow in Oxford. The ridges have remained undisturbed for centuries, but they provided a suitable scene for a scientific venture in the fifties: see J.L. Harper and G.R. Sager, "Some aspects of the ecology of buttercups in permanent grassland", *Proceedings. British Weed Control Conf.* (I) 1953, 256-63. Might we locate these writings, those buttercups, and the cattle that nibble on them, in current process?
6 See *CWL 15*, section 21.
7 Schumpeter, *History of Economic Analysis*, 1106.

> By the phrase, 'crossing the Rubicon', I mean this: however important those occasional excursions into sequence analysis may have been, they left the main body of economic theory on the 'static' bank of the river; the thing to do is not to supplement static theory by the booty brought back from these excursions but to replace it by a system of general economic dynamics.[8]

Later we will find that the dynamic of the stationary state is relatively unproblematic in regard to the demands it makes on the aggregate of the community's decisions. The dynamic of the evolutionary state, on the other hand, is massively problematic in that regard. What dynamic are we talking about here? Evidently, the dynamic of real economic process. Yet, more evidently, not the dynamic of real economic process: for real economic process is a matter of booms, slumps, crises, and we seem so far quite uninterested in these realities. Our analysis, then, must be viewed as normative. However, I urge you not to slip at this stage into a fog of reflection or discussion of moral sciences or value-focused investigations, but rather to return to the analogy from car driving introduced in the Prologue. An engineer or a driving instructor can be eloquent about the dynamics of a car: the driver, even the eloquent engineer, can persist in changing gears badly. I will yield to the temptation to include, at this early stage of our searching for system, some few further comments about normative analysis of the dynamic. Experts may view my brief suggestions as somewhat of a caricature: chapter five, on measurements, will deal with the matter more thoroughly. My remarks are meant to give a helpful orientation to the beginner.

There is a sense in which I can speak of the dynamics of a square block of wood down an inclined plane as normative. Math-

8 *Ibid.*

ematical physics provides a general solution, a second order differential equation specifying the motion down the plane that includes a general coefficient of friction and a general angle of inclination. The particular angle can be determined – the coefficient of friction is a more complex matter, but lets assume we have some estimate – and with set initial conditions one can come up with a series of positions and times for the wooden block. Will the block, or did the block, pass through these positions at the time indicated? Pretty well, if *other things* remain equal. A powerful fan blowing up the plane would make a difference.

I use this illustration because it brings to mind Galileo and the genius of his empirical focus. Stillman Drake notes that before Galileo there was no dearth of mathematical reasoning but "the systematic appeal to experience in support of mathematical laws comes after Galileo's time."[9] Drake notes the difficulty of believing this, and so goes on to describe the inadequate strategies of Tartaglia (1546), Cardano (1570), and Ubaldo (1577), in seeking out laws of force for bodies on inclined planes.

An adequate strategy clings to the essentials of the empirical. This, of course, is not a deductivist a priori stance: the essentials, or more properly in the early stages of investigation the relevant data, have to be coaxed out, sometimes against a persistent prior theoretic or mythic perspective. Think of Kepler's struggles with Tycho Brahe's observational results.[10] Think, if you are a victim of a first year course in economics based on the inadequate strategies of equilibrium theory, of the struggle you are having with the present approach. What we are doing here is coaxing out the relevant ele-

---

9 Stillman Drake, *Galileo Studies*, Ann Arbor, University of Michigan Press, 1970, 44.
10 The struggle led Arthur Koestler to write *The Sleepwalkers*. I suggest above thinking of the transition, but note that the key is to have some transitions of one's own that ground understanding by analogy. I give a couple of helpful instances at the beginning of chapter five, but your main analogue should be the sleepwalking that is necessary to move through this elementary text.

ments, and while as yet we have not focused on money and exchange, we will come in the next chapter to the problem of adding relevant differentiations of exchanges and rates of exchange. We are focusing on production for sale, and so obviously on buying and selling. But notice the oddness of our focus: we are trying to hold together the flows of production in a concretely coherent fashion, and over and around that holding, as it were, we will mesh the net of exchange flows.

Are we interested in the buying and selling at some time t? Only later, and always within our hold of the flows. Keep recalling Galileo's block on the inclined plane. One might hold the block in equilibrium by attaching twine and pulleying it over the top of the plane by a determined weight, but that would be an exercise in statics, not dynamics. So, with the massive devotion of Walras or Debreau, one can work out an elaborate market-place statics of the economy for time t. It does not, of course, have the validity of the statics in physics, a point worth puzzling over.[11]

Let us move a step further. Let us say that we have determined the positions, p_1 and p_2, of the block at times t_1 and t_2. There are, of course, the obvious candidates for this: the beginning and end of the run. Then, for one thing, we can find an infinity of laws that will put the block precisely in the two states. Only a subgroup of these laws, at most a lesser infinity, will put the block precisely at actual measured intervening times and corresponding positions. An empirical focus here, paradoxically, drives us to a fuller theoretic perspective – one might add Newton's drive to Galileo's – but one can slip off in other directions. One might hold to some sort of comparative statics, or one might cook up a differential equation (only after Newton and Leibnitz of course!) that gives correct results, even pointing to some *natural rate* as in the old theory of impetus.

What is important here is to get some sense of a parallel in

11 B. Lonergan discusses Walras' efforts in *CWL* 15. See the index, under *Walras*.

48

economics. I know that I have risked loosing you and your interest if you are a beginner, but bear with me. Perhaps you might skim along till we leave our digression and get back to the flows.

Consider a developing economy, perhaps a third world economy at mid-century. It is not going up some inclined plane of development, but in four years it has shown a growth of 16%: how *that* is measured is another matter. What has happened? Well, there is the Harrod-Domar growth equation: the growth in total output, g, will be equal to the savings ratio, s, divided by the capital-output ratio, k: $g = s/k$. Suppose the capital-output ratio is 3, that is, three units of capital are required to produce an additional unit of output. Then if 12% of total output is saved annually, $g = 12/3$, $g = 4\%$ annually. So, in four years we have 16% growth: the equation neatly gets us from t_1 to t_2. As neat a job as any done by Tartaglia. Does this sort of thing happen? Do people really take this stuff seriously? Let's hear it from the 1991 *British Encyclopedia*:

> Growth theory, particularly the Harrod-Domar growth equation, has been frequently applied or misapplied to the economic planning of a developing country. The planner starts from a desired target rate of growth of perhaps 4%. Assuming a fixed capital-output ratio of, say, 3, it is then asserted that the developing country will be able to achieve this target rate of growth if it can increase its savings to $3.4\% = 12\%$ of its total output. The weakness of this type of exercise arises from the assumption of a fixed capital-output ratio, which assumes away all the vital problems affecting the developing country's capacity to absorb capital and invest its savings in a productive manner. These problems include the central problem of the efficient allocation of available savings among alternative investment opportunities and the associated organizational and institutional problems of encouraging the growth of a sufficient

supply of entrepreneurs; the provision of appropriate economic incentives through a market that correctly reflects the relative scarcities of products and factors of production; and the building up of an organizational framework that can effectively implement investment decisions in both the private and the public sectors. Such problems, which generally affect the developing country's absorptive capacity for capital and a number of other inputs, constitute the core of development economics. Development economics is needed precisely because the assumptions of growth economics, based as they are on the existence of a fully developed and well-functioning modern capitalist economy, do not apply.[12]

My contention, of course, is that the Harrod-Domar equation, or various other Keynesian and Post-Keynesian growth models, do not apply either to advanced or backward economies. That contention has to be substantiated in the following chapters, but the systematic key lies in the effort of this chapter and it is firmly linked to the methodological key touched on in these present asides. The primary substantiation becomes a personal reality through following up on the invitation to hold with leisurely patience to the empirical focus. In chapter five and in the Epilogue I will add some further points regarding both twentieth century economics and deeper methodological issues of our empirical bent. The beginner may not find such pointers helpful, at least at first, so they are kept to a minimum here, and even in the later discussions. The economic expert, especially the neoclassical expert, may well find both the pointers and the pedagogical effort quite beside the point. Still, I have more than a sense that history is on the side of this analysis, including the

12 *Encyclopedia Britannica*, Economics, volume 13, 1991, 884.

history of economics, indeed, also contra-factual economic history.[13] And a final paragraph relating to this is worth adding here, before getting back to our plodding towards system.

WW Rostow's little book, *How It All Began: Origins of the Modern Economy*,[14] which follows half a dozen others by him on the same topic, brings out very nicely the importance of the role of science, invention and innovation as lifting the commercial revolution of the 16th, 17th and 18th centuries into the concrete possibilities of the British industrial take-off in the years that span the turn of the 19th century, 1783-1820. He writes in the conclusion of the difficulty of handling this history in the absence of an adequate framework of economic theory. He writes of the increasing need in our time of a perspective on and a mediation of invention and innovation. Indeed I suspect that he would regard it as an increasing demand in an economic sense.[15] He recalls, as I do now for the reader, Dr. Johnson's principle that when a man knows he is to be hanged in a fortnight it concentrates his mind marvellously: the global ills of the turn of the century should surely cause such concentration. However, with some oddball exceptions, invention and innovation have little place in standard economic theory.

For two hundred years now – from Adam Smith, through Marshall and Robertson, to Samuelson and Kaldor – economists have not been able to integrate satisfactorily the generation of major new technologies with the corpus of

13 Contrafactual history has emerged in recent decades as a serious and worthwhile venture: it asks 'what might have happened?'. You will find it interesting, when we deal with functional specialization in chapter five, to seek its proper location, not in history, but primarily in the seventh specialty of genetic systematics. See notes 26 and 33 of chapter five.
14 WW Rostow, *How It All Began. Origins Of The Modern Economy*, McGraw-Hill, New York, 1975.
15 *Ibid.*, 134ff.

economic theory. In dynamic income analysis economists have been driven to a variety of devices that would make technological change incremental and a function of demand or the level of investment. Alternatively, they have put it outside the frame of theory, as an exogenous variable. Even the case of increasing returns has been dealt with mainly, since Marshall, in terms of incremental change, representing improvements associated with the scale of output. There has been, quite literally, no place in formal theory for major inventions and innovations.[16]

The relation between a formal theory and historical analysis is a complex issue. The present little book struggles to give some indications of what might be considered a formal theory, with occasional helpful distractions about historical events. The historical research that would both reveal the need of the theory and bring forth its fruit is quite another matter, as footnote 13 above intimates. But it is worthwhile to draw attention to some points which Bernard Lonergan makes regarding the problem of presenting only a formal theory.

The objection he deals with is that he is offering a historical synthesis without historical research. He does not answer the objection by appealing, as he might have, to relevant historical research, but by noting that all historical study rapidly reaches the point where interpretation of data can no longer be determined by the data. So, in economic history, general conclusions depend much more on the validity of general principles of interpretation than on accuracy of factual detail. Such a point seems to be lurking in the reflections of Rostow noted above. Lonergan goes on to discuss the manner in which Keynes, in an appendix to his *General Theory*, brings his own economic theory to bear on the mercantilists, content in his discussion to go only to a standard work of research on the topic.

16 *Ibid.*, 226.

The legitimacy of the procedure is evident, for, if research is necessary to determine in detail what the mercantilists thought and did, it cannot claim any competence in judging whether the mercantilists were wise or foolish. That question is answered only by economic theory, and each theory will give its own answer: the classicists have theirs, the Marxists no doubt offer another, and Mr. Keynes has given us a third; nor is the cause of the divergence a difference in the factual data but a difference in the principles accepted by the judging mind. Accordingly, if we succeed in working out a generalization of economic science, we cannot fail to create simultaneously a new approach to economic history. Such an approach is already an historical synthesis.[17]

These are large claims for what we are attempting, but the fuller context and the distant projects hinted at should add motivation in our struggle. We digressed to talk of normative analysis, and types of inadequate analysis. Galileo's inclined plane will stay with you, I hope, as a helpful parallel. As in the case of the moving block, there may be winds and frictions that we must gradually take into account. These may be more than minor: a feather dropped from the Leaning Tower of Pisa does not accelerate down at 32 feet per second per second. But empirical method has to reach forward to handle all kinds of disturbance and deviations. In the case of the productive process in an exchange economy, our interest must be in specifying and discovering and cultivating normative surges, however battered they may be by the winds of human foolishness and malice.

Let us get back, then, to our beginner's investigation of the flows of the productive process.

17 *CWL 21*, chapter 1, section 3.

Two distinct flows have been identified as giving rise to an actual standard of living. The basic flow enters the standard of living through purchase of consumer goods. The surplus flow, again through purchases that remain to be discussed, enters lower level flows. We want now to spell out certain correspondences that will help both to advance the appreciation of the nature and distinctions of the flows and to give an initial notion of the possibilities and limitations of measurements of the flows and their relations.

We wish, first, to relate elements in the productive process with elements in the standard of living: wheat with bread, cattle with steaks, linen with shirts, cotton with dresses, steel with cars. The list I give here, in fact, is a list with which you may easily associate a point-to-point correspondence. One pound of cattle will correspond, roughly, to one pound of meat; one square foot of linen will correspond roughly to one square foot of shirt; etc. More broadly, one bale of cotton corresponds to a certain number, x, of dresses; one ton of steel corresponds to a certain number, y, of cars. There are, of course, other elements of the productive process that go into the dresses, shirts, steaks, cars, and you may find it interesting to diagram the complex of elements in each case, as best you can. Further, you may envisage taking the measure, so to speak, of each contributing element in order to bring out the rough correspondence and to note also the evident limitation: out of twenty yards of cloth of a certain width one may get 15 or 18 dresses, depending on cut, length, weave, etc. But there will not be any more cloth in the final dresses than was in the initial roll. A unit of cloth equals x dresses, where x has a certain range. It might help to think of the point-to-point correspondence we are examining by thinking rather of small-area to small-area. Allowing for remaining fragments, you can locate a small patch of the original cloth as a small patch of dress.

The higher correspondence of point-to-line should, paradoxically, help towards clarity regarding what we are at here and its importance. One can make, or procure, a spade, for unearthing potatoes. You are coming to grips with the higher correspondence when it is clear to you that the spade is used, but not used up, in digging a dinnerful of potatoes. One hopes, indeed, to dig this year's dinners and more than next year's dinners. The spade, then, corresponds to an indeterminate series of potato-diggings, and to this indeterminacy we must later return.

You should search out illustrations of these correspondences in areas familiar to you: there are new computer components, but not a new computer factory, for each new computer. The computer components are in point-to-point correspondence with computers; the factory is in point-to-line correspondence with the computer. What of the management of the factory, of the computer designer, of the assembly line worker, of the security guard? And what of higher order correspondences? You may even find it interesting to inflict on your friends the task of turning up real or imaginary examples of machine tools that call for point-to-surface, point-to-volume, or even higher correspondences.

It should already have occurred to you, from your examination of these illustrations, that what has been said of steel and cotton holds also for the activities and services involved in the various levels of the productive process. The rough correspondence, too, recurs: in providing wheat for bread, sowers and reapers, millers and bakers, deliverers and salespersons, can be more or less efficient. At all stages here there is need for wariness in holding to a search for function, for level of flow. Neither a type of factory nor a type of product need be identified with a definite level of the productive process. Consider the ordinary car. At first sight, it is evidently an element in the standard of living. Yet you can easily think of ways in which it can be part of the productive process at any level: a factor in a rental service, or in the sales management of machine tools. When one moves to consider institutions of production, one needs even more care: automobile, oil and power corporations provide indifferently for elements in the standard of living and in the various levels of flow. Such indifference is not a headache for the corporation accountant, but certainly it seems to point to difficulties in the task of arriving at a measured determination of elements in the various flows. But it is important to note that the difficulties, in the main, are not difficulties of classification, nor do they represent concrete confusions. A day in the life of an automobile, indeed the life of an automobile, is a determinate sequence and linkage of functions isomorphic with our specified flows. All this may seem overly complicated, but it is an unavoidable feature of the struggle towards understanding systematically. Chemical reactions are less complicated than economic reactions: a day in the life of a hydrogen molecule is not easy to follow, but it is – let's slip past quantum theory here – a determinate sequence and linkage of concrete realizations of the relations expressed by the periodic table. Chemistry, of course, is a respected complex science: is it not time for economics to move on from its daze of alchemy?

What about the life of a bus, a small private company bus? It would seem that our view of correspondence does not fit easily here. The bus is used, let us say, on a regular run rather than through full-load rentals. Then, some regular runs may even happen without passengers. Still, we can hold to our point-to-line correspondence here. The variability of passenger count resembles the variability of the number of dresses from a bale of cotton. There is a point-to-point correspondence between bus-miles and passenger-miles, not in some fixed ratio, but in the sense that the bus moves as often and as far as passengers move. Each day there is a determinate ratio (anything from 0:1 to 50:1 if the bus has 50 seats). Like the spade, the bus is not used up by the trip: so we arrive at a point-to-line correspondence of bus to passenger journeys.

Let us stay with our small bus company, something you may be familiar with whether you are in India, Africa or Nova Scotia. You can envisage the accounts being kept, estimates being made of durability, repairs being carried out, buses being maintained or replaced. Can you sort out these activities, and the goods involved, in terms of the flows? The problem of maintenance is obviously a recurring problem. To fit this activity and the goods involved into the flow-analysis, one has to think out the type of maintenance involved. Regular replacements, of engine, body or wheel parts, might be regarded as prolongations of production. Many features of maintenance seem closer to continued use: gassing up, oiling, washing, waxing, painting, rust-prevention. It would be interesting to follow up these questions while availing of an accountant's view of the bus-company. Our aim here is to reach some notion about the separability of descriptive units of accounting and of maintenance, so that sometimes maintenance is placed in correspondence with the use of equipment, sometimes it is placed in the higher correspondence of making of equipment. But always there is a distinct functional place for it, in so far as it is an element in the process of basic and surplus production.

Finally, our bus company can help us to make a very clear negative point which is central to our establishing the correspondences, and the indeterminacies, of point-to-point, point-to-line, point-to-surface, etc., between elements in the productive process and elements in the standard of living.

The company owner, whether in Halifax or in Uttar Pradesh, has a pretty fair idea of, anticipation of, the rhythms of replacement of buses. The idea and the anticipation are helped, of course, by the business being a family business. Generations of people and of buses can be remembered and identified. Precise numbers may even be available, in the McDonald style: a free ride was given to the 1,000,000th passenger on the bus affectionately named Ulla. Similarly, we had earlier the continued use of the new spade: one can proudly dig the first potato of the third year. But I insisted there, as I insist here, on an indeterminacy. Neither estimates nor anticipations nor records take away from this indeterminacy. One does not junk an old bus that kind treatment and luck leaves far from obsolete beyond one's best estimate. On the other hand, a new bus can leave the road, and the productive process, disastrously, and there are disasters like bankruptcy when a new highway or airway plunges the company into uselessness.

The point is that we are pushing towards a normative explanatory analysis of economic dynamics. That normative analysis will ground critical appraisal of macro and micro-economic estimates and expectations and propensities. It would obviously lose its critical legitimacy if it itself were based on estimates and expectations. So, one must hold to the on-going present fact of indeterminacy.

If you are innocent of present economic theory, the importance of this stand is most likely lost on you. But if you have had some slight brush with twentieth century theoretic contortions regarding measuring capital and its marginal productivity, *natural* rates of interest or profit or unemployment, etc. etc., then you may have some suspicion that we are closing some too-long-open phlogiston-door in economic theory. And if you are pushing forward in our fresh approach in spite of such a background or education, then you may have a growing sense of the mammoth task of replacing that pseudo-theoretic and its fallout in statistical analyses, economic forecasting, barren thesis-work, etc., with a theory and praxis adequate to our complex global needs.

I have continually and deliberately interrupted this introductory chapter with pointers towards this larger challenge. If you find them tiresome, distracting, then you have my repeated advice to slip quickly through them in order to focus on the central small challenge of this chapter. But I fancy that without the contextualizing, the central small challenge would become smaller in your estimation. At this stage you are clear that I wish to bring you to an appreciation of the need for, the significance of, the functional distinction of flows. But it may seem now too obvious, too trivial. I can assure you that it is not, but I prefer to rely on my distracting pointers to generate that assurance in you. We have lived through centuries of inadequate economic thinking and muddled or malicious economic policies. We may recognize that vaguely: the problem is to rise, as a community, to a clear-headed analytic recognition, and that rising, here and now, is unfortunately the humdrum elementary analytic struggle with ploughs and buses, with oil as it moves from earth to engine, with the rhythm of innovative flows of biotechnology that must be called forth to meet the demands of a teeming globe. It seems to me, then, not at all out of place to quote, in the centre of this early chapter, a basic summary page of Bernard Lonergan's economic work, *An Essay on Circulation Analysis:*

I have been looking at the dynamic structure of the industrial exchange economy. In it I have distinguished stationary states, the increasing returns that arise when the economy is tooling up for increased production but as yet is not thereby increasing living standards, and the decreasing returns that arise for investors when tooling up is tapering off and flow of consumer goods and services is increasing. I beg to note that such an analysis has not been tried and found wanting. Rather, to speak with Chesterton, it has been thought hard and not tried. What has been tried is roughly as follows:

(1) the emergence of industrial nations as creditors and others as debtors,

(2) the establishment of colonies and empires, their rivalries and wars,

(3) the rise of the arch-secularist, Marx, the industrial development of the U.S.S.R., its diplomatic and warlike achievements, and the moral support it enjoys from secularists everywhere,

(4) the welfare state with its substitution for a properly functioning basic phase and with its crumbling foundations in economic science, and

(5) the multinational corporations, their flourishing but off-shore economy, and the dual economies they effect not only in the underdeveloped countries but also in the U.S.[18]

Do you think the analysis is hard? I certainly do: as I remarked already, I spent five years of the seventies struggling with the original 1944 version of the work just quoted. Even if a community emerges, in these next decades, for which the analysis is a comfortable perspective, there is the further hard task of implementation. But that is not our concern here. Our concern is with the beginnings of that coherent perspective. So we return to that task, hopefully so inspired by a glimpse of the peak that the plodding becomes laced with visionary patience.

Our attention is now on the basic stage of the productive process which gives rise unmediatedly to the standard of living. Random particular elements in possible standards of living have already been used as illustrations: potatoes and poiteen, bus-journeys and bicycles, automobiles and restaurant services. I am assuming that the meaning of *standard of living* is sufficiently evident to you. But you will also have problems regarding that meaning: there are problems of inequality, locally and globally, and there are problems regarding what is to be considered as essential or desirable in human life. This poses the major problem of our time, the problem of locating these millennia in a fuller view of history, and determining the turn to the idea that would mediate richer human living.[19] A single instance can perhaps colour our concern.

---

18 *CWL 15,* section 22, "The Position of This Essay".
19 I have articulated the fuller view of history in P. McShane, "Middle Kingdom: Middle Man. T'ien hsia : i jen", chapter one of *Searching for Cultural Foundations,* University Press of America, 1984.

More than a billion people in our world today survive on less than $370 a year, while Americans, who constitute five per cent of the world's population, purchase fifty per cent of its cocaine. If the world's population, which has doubled in our lifetime, doubles again in the middle of the next century, how could anyone hope to escape the catastrophic consequences – the wrath to come?[20]

Such concern about human progress and decline should certainly be ours, but it is not our present concern. For present purposes, a standard of living is any actual order, dynamically emergent from the basic stage of the productive process. Central to such a standard of living may be the bread and circuses of a fading Rome, or the soaps, scandals, and Saturday hangovers of a present suburbia. Our concern is not with the quality of life, but with norms of the dynamics of the shifting of any standard towards what, somehow, is deemed better. The illustrations given throughout this text must be taken in this sense, as given, not approvingly, but factually or imaginatively.

The emergent standard of living, then, is an aggregate of rates at which goods and services move into the standard of living through purchase from the basic stage of the productive process. If we take a year as a unit, then there will be so much bread per year, so many passenger-miles per year, so much clothing a year, etc. There will be so much of each type of good or service every so often. We make no effort in this introduction to take on the problem of limits of types, varieties of bread, etc., but you can envisage a whole catalogue of elements, in whatever detail you like, with their associated rates. You can further envisage both the catalogue and the rates

---

20 T. Cahill, *How the Irish Saved Civilization. The Untold Story of Ireland's Heroic Role from the Fall of Rome to the Rise of Medieval Europe*, Doubleday, New York, 1995, 217.

changing from interval to interval. The aggregate of rates changes both quantitatively and qualitatively in successive time-intervals.

This aggregate of rates of emergence is not some systematic flow. Pounds of butter per year and bicycles are not related in any evident fashion. Notice also, if you are trying to hold this together imaginatively, that you must avoid thinking in terms of some end-of-interval emergence: rather, you must *time-slice* into the year's productive flow to capture what is emerging at that time. The emergence is distributed over the year.

Next, we wish to relate this emergence and its aggregate of rates to the aggregate of rates of production of goods and services that are in point-to-point correspondence with elements in the standard of living. Recall that this validly restricts our interest to basic production, but does not tie us to some rigid relationship. Butter is related to milk within the process by some algebraic equation, say, $aB = M$: so many grams of butter (a, *more or less*) are derived from a litre of milk; so many bicycles from so much metal; etc.

You have to focus now, imaginatively, on the goods and services in process, and this requires a fertile appeal to experience. There is a complex of small and large enterprises that leads from steel to bicycles, from cows to butter. Twined into this complex is the aggregate of rates of equipment-use, labour and management. The ultimate product is, say, a quantity of butter emergent simply from a store or more complexly – notice the mix of good and service – in a restaurant service. Let us take any such ultimate product, q_i, and trace its emergence within the process as distinct from its emergence from the process. In general we can claim that q_i emerges from j enterprises and that each enterprise contributes k factors of production: these factors, in each case, being in some organized mix of management, labour, use of capital equipment.

At this stage I suspect, if you are a normal commonsense reader seeking a perspective on what is going on, that you are being discouraged by this beginnings of complexity. Can you grin about it, bear it?! My effort here is not towards some popular and palatable deficient version of what the economic process involves, but towards an adequate introduction to a much-needed explanatory perspective. Already we have come some distance in following the functional distinction through in illustrations of economic process. The present further follow-through takes time, patience, imaginative energy, and it leads to a simple symbolization of an evident feature of our common experience of economic life:

$$q_i = \sum_j \sum_k q_{ijk}$$

The Σ (sigma) is just a Greek capital S: we have a double summation. One cannot go any distance in explanatory science without some such symbolization, and it may well be interesting to discover, here, why many people find symbols and formulae frightful: because the prior insightful climb is absent, was never invited. The lack of invitation points to a deeper cultural problem: undergraduates and graduates can move forward in a discipline – even in mathematics – through technical competence. They become abominable teachers, whether in university or in elementary school. The real issue here is whether you can become a non-abominable teacher: can you arrive at sufficient grasp of our formula to be able to invite understanding in a friend?

We began with a unit object-or-service, q_i. What you have to do, as learner, as potential teacher, is to take random illustrations of q_i, track back as best you can the enterprises, j, that are involved in the production, and pin down in a general way – numerical estimates are beyond us at the moment – the factors of production, k, of each enterprise. So, the carton of milk looks back to store employee and delivery trucking, to a milk-processing enterprise and a carton manufacturer, to sources of purification and paper, to farmers and foresters and chemists. And within all this there is the web of production and sales management. As you struggle with all this you will notice the amazing variety of unfinished goods and services that are associated with the single type, q_i. By unfinished I do not mean that the particular job is not done, that the particular service is not complete: I mean that the result is not part of the standard of living. A new empty milk carton is an element in the productive process.

At all events, with perhaps boxes for enterprises, circles for incomplete goods or services, diamonds for machines in use, and hosts of little arrows for transitions, patient diagramming and illustrations can lead you on to a competence in inviting others to grasp just how it is that $q_i = \sum_j \sum_k q_{ijk}$ neatly captures the complex flow.

Note that we have now two flows on the basic level, a flow within the process and a flow of emergence from the process. I have already warned about imagining the emergence being *at the end*. We are talking and thinking about a period, say a year, and the reality of daily milking and daily milk, petroleum tanker deliveries and gas station services. How are the two flows related? We have to aggregate, or sum the two flows. We have, say,

$Q_i = \sum q_i$ the total flow of ultimate products. We have – yes, it looks bad, but why worry about one more! –

$Q_{ijk} = \sum \sum \sum q_{ijk}$ the total flow of factors of production on the basic level.

We have aggregated here two quite different sets of rates of different goods-services, so certainly there is no question of an identity between the two summations. You might like to check this out with some simple *basket of consumer goods*. But obviously – or not so obviously to you? – the two summations are related: the aggregate of rates within the process are surely tightly related to the aggregate of rates of emergence of goods and services. One expects, for instance, that they will increase or decrease together in a closely related fashion. What more can be said? What is missing, you have perhaps already noticed, is some common measure for ultimate products and the contributions to ultimate products, and you are perhaps impatient for the introduction of such a measure, money. That is the topic of the next chapter. So, all we have at this stage is an equivalence that can become a measured relationship. But we must note two features of this equivalence. First, there can be mistakes and accidents at any stage in the productive process: we have all, perhaps, at some time, ended up at the check-out counter with a leaky carton which the sales clerk puts aside. There can be breakdowns, various wastages, slips of management. Secondly, if you have done some diagramming it will be evident to you that there is a scattering of lags. If the organization of the various enterprises is stable, then there may be regular lags, but the general case is a complex variable pattern of lags. Each case, however, is determinate: with sufficient labour one might catalogue time periods of production and time-lags of the contributions to particular types of end-product.

So, we have two equivalent aggregates of rates: the basic stage of the productive process; the emergent standard of living. They vary together, quantitatively and qualitatively. But their variations are not measured. To turn the equivalence into a mathematical equality requires the work of chapter three.

There should be no great difficulty, now, in doing something similar with regard to the first level surplus stage, or any higher level of surplus activity. You have to change the illustrations of complete and incomplete goods and services, and you have to bear in mind that now you are not dealing with an emergent standard of living, consumer goods and services, but with the emergent goods and services that pass into use in the next lowest stage of the process. What emerge – trucks, oil tankers, management skills – become means of production. One can talk about the consumption of the productive stages in a broad sense: produced goods and services are consumed by producers.

At all events, we find an equivalence that parallels the equivalence discovered for the basic level. Allowing for lags and mistakes, we can recognize the relation between an ultimate product, q_i, and the contributing factors of production, as that of a double summation.

Before turning to the shifting of such equivalences into measured equivalences through the introduction of a monetary counterflow, it is as well to focus again on the main insight of our analysis so far, how the surplus levels and the basic level relate. You can still exploit our initial illustrations, the invention of plough or basket, to come to grips more accurately with this relationship.

First we note the difference between a short-term acceleration of the productive process and a long-term acceleration. For a short-term acceleration there is merely a change of pace. Inventory-reduction with a change of pace of sales is a simple instance, but more broadly there is more efficient use of existing capital equipment, management, labour. There is a limited surge without added technology or new types of technology: so, the rate of emergence of ploughs, for instance, goes up. In a long-term acceleration, there is more than a change of pace. It may, indeed, not involve new types of technology, but simply be the introduction of more capital, with concomitant changes in other factors. The additional capital obviously comes from the next highest level of production: we will get back to that. But the acceleration can also be due to the introduction of more efficient capital, even with an orientation towards eventual novel consumer goods. The bright idea has emerged, for instance, of superseding the horse plough, or more remotely, there can be the biochemical idea at a higher surplus level grounding new layers of recurrence-schemes right down to new consumer possibilities in vegetable diet. In the latter case, one must envisage layered and lagged surges on the various levels and we will presently try to capture this symbolically. For the moment, however, we may simply follow common usage and speak of widening capital or deepening capital as grounding long-term acceleration: widening involving only an increase of the quantity of old technology, deepening requiring the introduction of novel technology.

As you think this out and illustrate it, it is obviously best to hold to the complexity already arrived at: the accelerations we are considering involve accelerations within the realities caught by our double summations. You can imagine here all sorts of problems of lags, sluggishness, bottlenecks, psychological and local inelasticities, whatever. You may even be familiar with turnpike theorems. But the main problem is to remain concrete in your perspective and attention. We are not model-building: we are trying to home in on what actually happens, however sloppily it happens.

If you thus follow up details of either our elementary illustrations or illustrations of your own, through reading or imagination, you can move towards a refined notion of a long-term acceleration of the whole productive process. You may note, for instance, how a long-term acceleration calls forth short-term accelerations. You will note, too, that not every large innovation fits the bill. I chose the *plough-island* both for its simplicity and for its plausibility. The plough-shift in such a community would not be a minor disturbance: one can envisage shifts in horse training and horse racing, land structuring and leather-making, cattle raising and barn-building, eating and drinking. Such major shifts occur in modern economies: the railway transformed nineteenth century British commerce; the automobile did something similar in twentieth century Spain, and may do the same in twenty-first century China.

Again, you may think of the achievements of advanced economies being copied by backward economies, regularly in terms of five-year plans or ten-year plans. In advanced economies one thinks of revolutions: industrial, transportational, informational, whatever. We considered, in broad but concrete terms, short-term acceleration and long-term acceleration at any level of the productive process. It is important to advert regularly to the perspective of our analysis contained in the word *concrete*.[21] We are not dealing with a model,

---

21 Concreteness, all-inclusiveness, is quite a tricky topic regarding the reach of mind, minding, and the curious reduplicative minding of minding. I can at best simply point you towards Lonergan's view of metaphysics expressed in *Insight*.

but with the reality of what is involved in, say, a short term acceleration of basic production. The shoe factory is the same, but there is a taking up of slack that you must envisage as concretely as you can: different management energies, a new pace of labour and machine usage. It may be centred in sales management and the reduction of inventory.

Let us follow up the change in the basic productive process that is consequent on a shift in the first surplus stage. It should not be too difficult to grasp that the *purely* long term acceleration of basic production can be thought of as the actual long-term acceleration less the acceleration, if any, due to taking up slack. What is this part of the acceleration due to? Obviously, to a flow into usage on the basic level of the products of the surplus level. But here again we must distinguish something like a *pure* flow. The total flow from the surplus level, after all, includes the flow of replacement and maintenance. In a stationary state, that total flow is nothing but a flow of replacement and maintenance. In a surge, the total flow becomes larger.

Let us try for a convenient symbolization of all this.

Let us call B_s the rate of production of the surplus level that is required for replacement and maintenance, and the total rate of production, or velocity of production, vel_s. Then $vel_s - B_s$ is the 'pure' velocity of production, in the sense that $vel_s - B_s$ is over and above replacement and maintenance: it is related to the *pure* acceleration of basic production.

Basic production's short-term acceleration can be symbolized as A_b: then if we call the full basic acceleration acc_b, we can write the *pure* acceleration of basic production as $acc_b - A_b$. It is this that relates to $vel_s - B_s$. Can we get the relation into an equation, in spite of our postponing the establishment of a precise standard of measurement? Whatever the measure, we can view the relation as determined by some multiplier which we may call k_s, so we can write:

$$\mathrm{acc}_b - A_b = k_s[\, \mathrm{vel}_s - B_s \,] \text{ or}$$
$$\mathrm{acc}_b = A_b + k_s[\, \mathrm{vel}_s - B_s \,].$$

Before reflecting further on the meaning of this equation, the time element must be considered. Recall our regular illustration of the shift from a spade culture to a plough culture. There are obvious time-lags in getting the long-term acceleration of the basic stage underway. The new plough emerges prior to the results of its use. Let us settle for some unspecified lag-time, a. Then we can give our equation the following final form:

$$\mathrm{acc}_b(t) = A_b + k_s[\, \mathrm{vel}_s(t - a) - B_s \,].$$

The equation helps us to hold down our discoveries. In a stationary state, there is no acceleration of basic production, neither short-term acceleration nor long-term acceleration. The two parts of the right side of the equation are each zero. If there is an acceleration of basic production, then it can occur in two ways, or a mix of two ways. Again, this is clear from the right side of the equation.

We can reach a more general result by adjusting our labelling. Instead of subscripts b and s, we write 1 and 2: then we can add equations with subscripts 3, 4, etc., for the next surplus levels. So, we can arrive at a set of equations, with lag-times included that I will sort out immediately:

$$\mathrm{acc}_1(t) = A_1 + k_2[\, \mathrm{vel}_2(t - a) - B_2 \,]$$
$$\mathrm{acc}_2(t - a) = A_2 + k_3[\, \mathrm{vel}_3(t - b) - B_3 \,]$$
$$\mathrm{acc}_3(t - b) = A_3 + k_4[\, \mathrm{vel}_4(t - c) - B_4 \,]$$
etc.

The time-lags that are included are not difficult to sort out. We already had the lag a. The first surplus level acceleration at time t – a depends on the higher surplus production at an earlier time, t – b. The lag is t – a – (t – b) = b – a. So we have a series of lags: a, b – a, c – b, etc.

The equations, as I mentioned, bring together our discoveries. But if you are not in the habit of handling this type of symbolization, it can be quite a task to work towards *reading the equations* comfortably with the concrete comprehension that our struggle aims at. Without the symbolization you can still grasp in some manner what it expresses. Any level can accelerate on its own in short-term fashion. This can occur on the basic level without immediate related changes on the surplus level. But notice the effect of a short-term acceleration occurring on the first surplus level. With a lag, it gives rise to a long-term acceleration on the basic level of production: there is basic capital-widening. More generally, one can envisage a short-term acceleration on a higher level: then, with lags, there will be a series of long-term surges on each of the lower levels.

I have held to the word *surge* here because it has no overtones such as *cycle* or *wave* has, overtones of ups-and-downs, of booms and slumps. What is envisaged is a series of lifts that end with a permanent lift to the standard of living.

While booms and slumps do not belong in the limiting ideal of our *normative* economics – though their avoidance is the major challenge envisaged by this analysis – obsolescence and innovative replacement certainly do. They were a major concern of the economist Joseph Schumpeter, but they are also factors intended by Lonergan's analysis.[22] How they are made explicit in that analysis is

22 Among the handwritten scribbles (probably early forties) in the Lonergan Archives, Toronto, is the following note: "My real and my circulation phases involve no distinction between growth (mere increase in size) and development (new productive combinations). For Schumpeter these two are specifically distinct – the new production functions create new situations that increase enormously the average of error and bring about the cycles. However, the ideas of capital, credit, interest, etc., that Schumpeter advances appear more clearly and more generally and in more detailed a fashion. The relevance of Schumpeter's insistence on

a complex question. Like the question of planetary disturbances, it is best left out of an introductory text. The interested reader can find some leads in the work of the Australian economist, Peter Burley.[23] A further complexification occurs when one takes account of the historical and geographical intersection of varieties of innovation: again, a topic for more advanced work.[24] The inclusion of symbolism in these last few pages is itself a complexification which may well have discouraged you. It is quite a task to move into this context without benefit of an enlightened community: Newton's equations were once a disconcerting challenge in physics. But at least you have an impression now of *natural* economic surges. Next we will tackle the fundamental problem: what rhythms of financial flows are required to carry these surges forward successfully. You are already too well aware, perhaps, that the required rhythms are altogether remote from our present ethos of government and profit-

development as opposed to growth is in the concatenation of the phases, e.g. Schumpeter's development can take place in my static phase if $DQ_n > O$ and if the new combinations are continuously offset by equal liquidations of former enterprises."

23 See Peter Burley, "A von Neumann Representation of Lonergan's Production Model", *Economic Systems Research* 1, 1989, 317-330; "Evolutionary von Neumann Models", *Journal of Evolutionary Economics* 2, 1992, 269-280; Peter Burley and Laszlo Csapo, "Money Information in Lonergan-von Neumann Systems", *Economic Systems Research* 4, 1992, 133-141. Such work, however, must be considered critically in the context of the projects sketched in chapter five below.

24 In an earlier reflection on the topic, I made the following comment: "There is no doubt that the solar system, even macrodynamically speaking, involves an aggregate of bodies. Was, then, the solution of the two-body problem irrelevant? Again, there is no doubt that tidal waves are not sinusoidal. Should we then drop the dynamic question and settle for some equivalent of photography and comparative statics? Or should we not make sense of elementary rhythms, momenta, etc., acknowledging that we are only paving the way for such developments as Fourier analysis?", *Lonergan's Challenge to the University and the Economy*, University Press of America, 1980, 118-9; second edition, Axial Press, forthcoming.

making, when "orthodox economics is in many ways an empty box."[25] But that very emptiness should ground not merely a short-term pessimism but the long-term optimism that was mentioned in the Prologue. To Lonergan's remark, quoted there at footnote 2, I replied by recalling the title quoted there at footnote 3. The second million years is on our side. Lonergan's economics is not really a paradigm shift, but a beginning. So it seems worthwhile to conclude this difficult chapter with a lengthy echo of his hope of over fifty years ago:

> Nor is it impossible that further developments in science should make small units self-sufficient on the ultra-modern standard of living to eliminate commerce and industry, to transform agriculture into a super-chemistry, to clear away finance and even money, to make economic solidarity a memory and power over nature the only difference between high civilization and primitive gardening.
>
> But we are not there yet. And for society to progress towards that or any other goal it must fulfil one condition. It cannot be a titanothere, a beast with a three-ton body and a ten-ounce brain. It must not direct its main effort to the ordinary product of the standard of living but to the overhead product of cultural implements. It must not glory in its widening, in adding industry to industry, and feeding the soul of man with an abundant demand for labour. It must glory in its deepening, in the pure deepening that adds to aggregate leisure, to liberate many entirely and all increasingly to the field of cultural activities. It must not boast

---

25 Paul Ormerod, *The Death of Economics*, Faber and Faber, London, 1994, ix. The first half of Ormerod's book is a criticism of present economic theory and practice; the second half contains his suggested solution, which certainly does not lay the axe to the root.

of science on the ground that science fills its belly. It must not glue its nose to the single track of this or that department. It must lift its eyes more and more to the more general and more difficult fields of speculation, for it is from them that it has to derive the delicate compound of unity and freedom in which alone progress can be born, struggle, and win through.[26]

26 *CWL 21,* chapter 2, section 9, conclusion. Throughout these two chapters you may have become increasingly puzzled about the absence of any consideration of employment and unemployment. (Consider the title of the work cited in the next footnote!). The above quotation may, perhaps, give you the beginnings of an answer, but to reach for it requires the concrete creative fantasy that I write of in the Epilogue.

Beyond The Casinos

3

"When the capital development of a country becomes a by-product of the activities of a casino, the job is likely to be ill-done."[1]
Keynes, of course, was writing of the stock exchange activities of
his day. He could hardly have anticipated the activities of sixty years
later. Of that casino in America, Kevin Phillips writes:

> By the mid-1990s the bond market – and the overall financial
> sector – had become a powerful usurper of control over eco-
> nomic policy previously exercised by Washington. Reckless
> government indebtedness is the conventional explanation.
> Yes, but there is also another reason: since the early 1970s, the
> clout of the financial sector has exploded into today's trillion-
> dollar, computer-based megaforce. Through a 24 hour cascade
> of electronic hedging and speculating, the financial sector has
> swollen to an annual volume of trading 30 or 40 times greater
> than the dollar turnover of the 'real economy'.[2]

As well as that casino one may think of the entire Las Vegas
of the money business, a web that includes the spectrum of banking in the new world of E-cash, the IMF, multinational liquidity,

1 J.M. Keynes, *The General Theory of Employment, Interest and Money, Collected Works*,
volume 7, Macmillan , London, 1971, 159.
2 Quoted in *Time*, September 26, 1994, 43, in a pre-publication excerpt, "Fat City,"
from *Arrogant Capitalism: Washington, Wall Street and the Frustrations of American Poli-
tics*, Little Brown and Co., 1994.

third and second world indebtedness, and the casino of government. And this casino was in operation centuries before such innovations as Internet's Offshore Casino.

To what extent is international development, or rather its frustration, really a by-product of unenlightened and self-interested money business, monetary and fiscal policy? I hope that we will get some distance towards the context of an answer to this question by the end of chapter four. I raise the question here, however, because part of the brilliance of the economic analysis of Bernard Lonergan is the precise locating of the casino, the Las Vegas, and its replacement. In the previous chapter we moved towards a set of equations which held, suggestively, the meaning we had reached for the productive process and its surges. In the present chapter we move towards a diagram (see page 92) that is magnificently suggestive of the rescuing of economic policy from the gamblers. You can check it immediately, even with little comprehension, and recognize something like a baseball pitch. The pitcher's mound becomes for Lonergan the locus of what I identified above as the larger casino, in a normative context. What of the bases? A vague pointer, even at this stage, is useful. You must avoid a notion of going round the bases, and think of two dominant circulations: a circulation between third and second base that we will associate with the process of surplus production; a circulation between home plate and the first base that we will associate with basic production.

Some of my readers will be unfamiliar with baseball. They will be relieved to hear that the diagram has nothing to do with baseball: the essentials of it are five zones with connecting arrows. My own knowledge of baseball is so limited that I had to check an encyclopedia to name the bases properly. Until my wife persuaded me to watch the Blue Jays win something or other last year I had never witnessed a game, and still resonate with Bob Newhart's comic description of the game.

But I may carry forward the allusion to baseball by noting that our attention in this chapter is initially on the four bases. Our interest is in the monetary flows that correspond to the flows of production discussed in the previous two chapters. Furthermore, we will continue to restrict ourselves to considerations of an isolated island. So, we are dealing with the internal and essential operations of any modern exchange economy: by internal I am excluding transnational operations; by *essential* I am excluding government operations. Considering government operations as *unessential* certainly seems peculiar: the meaning will emerge gradually.

So, we continue in the perspective of the previous chapter, where we already noted that the productive process included sales. What is not sold must then be considered an unfinished product, or else it is outside the productive process like Robinson Crusoe's food or the self-sufficiency of a commune. In so far as a sub-group has no dealings, in sales or the equivalent, with those in the exchange economy, it is not part of the economy. Put simply, the economy of our interest is the making and doing of things that other people want badly enough to pay for. The last phrase brings to mind two things, scarcity and possessions: very obviously, exchange at a price involves possession, and wanting badly has some relation to scarcity. Neither of these aspects of exchange will distract us from our main objective, to reach an appreciation of the financial flows that might match the productive flows we have been investigating.

You have reached some grasp of the fact that, in any advanced economy, there are one or more surplus levels, a basic level, and an emergent standard of living. The emergent standard of living is consumer to the basic level, the basic level is consumer to the surplus level, and so on. We found that the rate of consumption, at any level, has the form of a double summation of the activities that went towards the product consumed: activities of enterprises drawing on factors of production and moving the product towards completion. This gives us our starting point for considering what we might imagine as the counterflows, rates of payment that correspond to the rates of productive flows in the complexity of their staggered summations.

Before we reflect on rates, however, we must arrive at systematic precision with regard to classes of payments. The first precision takes us back to the starting point of this chapter, and may recall for you stray problems of the previous chapters. There are activities that have financial equivalents yet they are not strictly part of, or not totally part of, the current productive process. The most obvious instance of this is the transfer of static wealth, which is already outside the process. Eve owns a private home which she sells to Esther, who pays outright. There is a transfer of title of ownership and of money, but these activities do not belong in, are not constitutive of, current process. If you are thinking this out concretely, of course, likely enough from your own experience, you will note layers of complexity. Banks and real estate agents are involved, mortgaging and taxation lurk in the wings. Features of these activities can certainly be identified as belonging to the productive process. But these features, and these connections, do not negate the essential feature of the transaction which is that the transfer of ownership is not a move along any productive process. So we can say that the correlative financial transfer is not operative in the productive process: it is merely redistributive. This gives you an initial glimpse of the fundamental division of payments into operative and redistributive.

We took an obvious instance of a non-operative payment. Later we will tackle more complex instances. But you may already be anticipating a main result of the division: however large and active the stocks and commodities casino may be, really or symbolically, those activities are not essentially constitutive of the productive process.

Before dealing further with redistributive payments, we had best home in on what were named operative payments. In chapter two we used the image of a counterflow. A counterflow to what?

Obviously to the flows of goods and services, and to hold to our concrete perspective it is best to keep in imagination and mind the fruit of our struggle towards layers of double summations. If you are not mathematically inclined, you may be put out by this reference back. Then think of this double summation as a help, to hold together your growing understanding of the process. And get yourself a simple illustration of it. Recall the milk industry. The farmer, certainly, may sell the milk directly to particular customers that consume it. But in our advanced economy there is a clustered line of enterprises involved between farmer and final purchaser. And of course the final purchases in some cases will not be milk but cheese or chocolate. The use of the word *final* here leads us to specify the most evident operative payment: it is final in the sense that it takes the product out of the process of production. It completes the product: an unsold product, an unpaid service, is not complete in the view of the present analysis. When it is paid for it is consumed, economically, even if it is spilled on the way home.

Each level has its specific final payment: on the basic level it moves the product or service into the possession of the consumer. On higher levels it moves the service or product into use on a lower level. Again, if you are thinking this through concretely, you will be noting oddities: you need only recall the slogan, *buy now, pay later*, or advert to your capacity for *plastic loans*. We must patiently put questions of lags, instalment payments, etc. on hold.

A point worth repeating, since it does persist in troubling the beginner, is that our focus is away from the possession that is linked with payment. You notice here that I avoid talking about possessors in the usual fashion of economic texts: workers, capitalists, rentiers, etc. We spoke of Eve and Esther: someone is selling something to someone else when there is a sale even though the *someone* can be quite an obscure entity in the dealings of large corporations. Do not let the *someones* distract you: our focus throughout remains on functions rather than, so to speak, on functioners or functionaries.

As well as functions, however, we now have a measure of functions, of activities, of goods and services. Even before we move on to complete our classification of payments, it is evident enough, by considering our final payments, that they are proportionate to the volume of production, that they immediately provide a common measure of the process, a measure intrinsic to each element as completed.[3] But, please, do not let the word *intrinsic* lead you off into some strange metaphysic. Marxists may speak of labour theories of value, Popes and trade unions can wax eloquent on just wages, governments can talk of suitably fixed prices. Our stand, once again, is empirical. The question of justice, however, is not shelved: but the particular sacred and secular related questions require the full context of an answer to the macroeconomic question, What is the just pattern of national and global economic surges?

Back, then, to our identification of classes of payments. We name initial operative payments the payments made within a given enterprise to the factors of production contributing to that enterprise. The payments reach a wide variety of contributing factors. In any standard accounting text that variety is specified in descriptive detail but here it is sufficient to advert to commonly-recognized types of payment: the spectrum of payments to employed individuals, to banks and types of shareholders, to depreciation, to sinking and other funds.

Recall now our double summation that points, in general, to a cluster of enterprises, some of which are involved in a temporal sequence of partially completing the product. As well as each deal-

3 A problem lurks here regarding measure and prices. See, for example, the comment of Kaldor at note 5 of the Prologue. As I indicate at note 1 of chapter 5, I am avoiding discussion of the measuring of prices (including the prices of money and estimates of fixed capital assets) in this elementary text. I rely on the beginner's commonsense notion that e.g. basic expenditure is some aggregation of multiples of basic prices and basic quantities. Problems relating to pricing are extensively discussed in Lonergan's two volumes on economics, *CWL 15, 21*: see the index under *price*.

ing with factors of production, each deals with the enterprise or enterprises prior in the sequence. These payments are, as it were, internal to the process from raw potentialities to emergence through final sales and payments. They are the payments that effect the transition of the incomplete product from one enterprise to the next, so they are suitably called transitional payments. Their *disappearance* in our analysis of rates and circuits will, I hope, not surprise you: if it does, you must pause over the note below.[4] We have, then, three types of operative payments, payments that recur with the recurrence of productive routines. Each type of payment occurs on each of the levels of production. Here is where you may note a departure from accounting descriptions. It would be interesting for you, if you wished a leisurely and fruitful departure here from our analysis, to tackle some exercises in functional distinction, exercises that will eventually grow into a major task of reorientation of economic categorizations and measurements. Accountants, indeed present economists, are not in our ballpark. We are back to the problem of determining the break-up of payments within our odd perspective of point-to-point, point-to-line, etc., relations. You will find that it does actually break up both standard payments and normal enterprises. But this painful struggle in relation to both present and historical data, always part of a major theoretic shift, is not our present concern. Our present concern is that you grasp as plausible, indeed as necessary, the distinction between the three types of operative pay-

4 The problem is a standard one in first year texts: excluding 'double entry' for 'intermediate goods': see Gordon, *Macroeconomics*, Harper Collins, 1993, 33-34. We have been using milk enterprises as an illustration, so you might think this out in terms of the journey of a litre of milk as it is bought from the farmer at, say, $.50, and moves to processor, to supplier, to grocer, to consumer, who pays, say, $1.50. The key point is to grasp the need to exclude the payments in between, the receipts of the middle-businesses. But your challenge is to think this out concretely, in terms of the boxes, circles, diamonds, etc. suggested in chapter 2. There really is no other way to come to grips with the complexity of payments that matches the complexity of the productive process.

ments, initial, transitional and final, and the distinction between such payments that is rooted in our division of the process of production into layers. So, we have initial operative basic payments to factors of basic production; there are transitional basic operative payments; there are final basic operative payments that move the product into the standard of living. And so on, for other levels.

Besides the operative payments there are the redistributive payments already illustrated by the clear instance of the resale of a private house. But not all instances are clear. Above I listed payments to banks among initial operative payments. Perhaps you were alert enough to have suspicions regarding that inclusion? One has to determine precisely what is paid to the bank. The bank enters the productive process as an enterprise rendering a variety of services. Payments for its services, as in any other enterprise, meet the requirements of its initial payments. So, consider the most evident payment in banking: interest. If another enterprise has borrowed from the bank, it will meet interest payments. These interest payments are initial payments for the enterprise, basic or surplus depending on the function within that enterprise. But to the bank they are final payments. Such final payments to the bank meet, among others, the banks initial payments of interest to depositors. What of that bulky element, the borrowed money or the deposited money? It is that bulky element that falls, in its payment either way, within our redistributive function. You may well find it useful here to try the analogy from the early instance of transfer of ownership, or, better perhaps, consider the process of renting. But please, do not slip into that cloudy zone of some economists, the *reward of waiting*, turning interest and its fluctuations into mysteries of expectations or *animal spirits* or monetary policy. Only in chapter five and the epilogue will there be some brief comments on the issues of interest and profit and prices and of their fluctuations. Here we are pushing for simple explanatory classifications. You may feel that we are hair-splitting and adding enormous difficulties to economic accounting. Perhaps it is best to claim that, yes, we are splitting hairs necessarily along functional lines, and, yes, we must foresee a complex reorientation of economic accounting. Again, I would recall that such discomforting shifting is a feature of scientific revolution. Physicists were quite discomforted by the demands of Schroedinger and Heisenberg. Zoologists are at present comfortable with reductionist tendencies in zoological accounting: to account for animals according to functions of sensibility is a foreign and frustrating but necessary shift.[5]

What has been said of banks applies also to various other types of operations that involve transfer of money, such as the business of insurance or pension funding or various government operations. Any of these may be taken up as an exercise in grasping the nature and the reach of our distinctions.

In this short introductory work it would be out of place to seek for refinements of the species of redistributive payments. But such refinements will be necessary developments of the analysis. In undergraduate programmes they would be handled in various other courses, such as the course on varieties of financial transactions. For our purposes it is sufficient to acknowledge the general function associated with the centre circle of the diagram on page 92.

Still, it is as well to draw on your own experience, imagination and interests here to keep the concrete perspective of our introductory searchings, giving that focus to the next effort of getting to grips with the flows of the classes of payments. So, you may reflect on our initial quotation from Keynes regarding the casino: I would like you to begin to suspect that the gambling goes far beyond the market in stocks, commodities, monies. Indeed, such market gamblings shrink in significance when one locates properly, eventually by means of the systematic analysis we are struggling towards, the gamblings recommended by Keynes himself and by followers

5 I have discussed this matter in "Zoology and the Future of Philosophy", chapter three of *The Shaping of the Foundations*, University Press of America, 1976.

of Friedman, the gamblings of government spending and taxing, gamblings with prime rates and money supplies, the gamblings of *The Money Lenders*: "We have some chips in every game in town... In a spectrum of 156 countries there are always going to be three or four in trouble."[6]

One helpful introductory way to reach the significance of a transaction is to note to what extent it is related to old stock or someway (with people like Mobutu in Zaire it may never get there!) to new stock. With old stock, the gambling activities can be as harmless as Eve selling her house to Esther. The transaction is an instance of the secondhand trade, but resembles more Eve selling Esther her factory, or perhaps her farm when *natural resources* are being traded. Just as in banking, there are operative payments for services of traders, but the bulk financial transfer is redistributive.

The move towards new stock is another matter, bringing up the large problem of the nature of investment and carrying us into the zone of what I might call significant gambling, fundamentally unenlightened or malicious manipulation of the normative global rhythms of the processes of production. In our concrete approach it is necessary, however difficult, to try to bear such problems in mind as we begin our struggle towards an understanding of the rates of flow of operative and redistributive payments in an isolated economy. So I think it worthwhile to preface that effort with a lengthy and sound quotation from a post-Keynesian source. The drive of our analysis could be said to be towards a theory of investment. The quotation poses the problem in concrete complexity. Your reading at this stage will be impressionistic; by the end of chapter five you should be able to read it with a critical eye, having then in mind the central question, To what extent can we decisively evaluate uncertain prospects from a systematic response to past experience that goes beyond conventions of self or national interest?

6 Anthony Sampson, *The Money Lenders. Bankers and a World in Turmoil.* The Viking Press, New York, 1981, 145. This work will be referred to henceforth as *Sampson.*

In modern capitalist economies it is impossible to construct a theory of investment that is independent of the portfolio preferences of businessmen and financial managers. A decision to invest necessarily implies simultaneously a decision to acquire a tangible asset and to issue a financial asset. Since the future is essentially unknowable, and yet decisions with long-run implications nevertheless must be undertaken, real world businessmen are forced to rely on conventions. Past experience is widely believed to be the common basis for determining attitudes and responses to uncertainty and risk, and so it is for the evaluation of the uncertain prospects which attend financial values and investment decisions. This is reflected not only in changing stock market values, but also in the changing asset and liability structures of firm and household balance sheets. The ratio of debt servicing charges to net profits, leverage (debt to equity) ratios, and the term structure of private debts all reflect the views of businessmen and bankers as to what is permissible, and these standards of permissiveness change systematically in response to past experience.[7]

Encouraged darkly by this heady global problem, we move now from the identification of classes of payments to a specification of their flow, or perhaps at this stage it may be as well to speak of their circulation. The previous quotation, however, remains as a challenge and a touchstone. You will find it useful, for instance, to return to it as soon as you feel slightly comfortable about the way in which diagrams in this chapter bring the monetary functions into focus. It will take chapter four to give the full context. But you will always have the same problem as you had with Gordon's categorizations in chapter one: it is the general problem of trying to fit descriptive classification into an explanatory functional mould.

7 Basil J. Moore, "Monetary Factors", *A Guide to Post-Keynesain Economics*, edited by A. Eichner, Sharpe, New York, 1979, 128.

We begin with final payments, identified as on both basic and surplus levels. These payments remove products from the productive process: if the products are surplus, their use becomes part of a lower level process. The payments are final in that sense, and we have already made mention of the exceptions to this finality, covered by the broad category of the second hand trade. The final payments themselves, however, do not *escape* the process. The flow of final payments moves on in the process. Previously we used the metaphor of counterflow: the metaphor misleads if it is not stretched to mean a flow *against* the flow of goods and services that also circulates. The stretching must reach further, moreover, to escape the imagining of a simple circular flow of payments, of money. The task ahead of us, indeed, is to reach a precise understanding and imaging of the flows of payments that would 'satisfy' the flows and surges of the process of production.

Another difficulty we face is the anonymity and flexibility of the flowing of payments. I am using the word *anonymous* in a very odd sense, but perhaps it brings to mind the anonymous donor or donation, to which you may add the idea of a non-directed donation intimated by the word *flexibility*. Perhaps you are already getting used to this peculiarity of our analysis: so, while we acknowledge possession as being a characteristic of payment, we are not interested in, nor distracted by, who pays. We are interested in how the money functions, and that has already been given sufficient meaning by our reflections on classes of payments. The money will function in meeting the flow of basic production or in meeting the flow of surplus production.

The meaning of the flexibility of money will gradually emerge, but perhaps some reflection on the money poised in your purse or pocket would help our concrete focus before we move on to other types of payments. Notice that this concrete focus is the necessary economic focus but it will be as difficult, or indeed more difficult, for economists to maintain that focus as it is for you as a beginner.

At all events, our analysis includes the money poised in your purse or your pocket. Where did it come from? Where is it going? Let us answer the first question generically by accepting that it is income – salary, pension cheque, whatever – and reflect on it as it is poised, undetermined, as you read. By the end of the day you may have bought groceries with some of it, deposited some of it in a savings account, spent some of it on the equivalent of a new last for a shoe-repair business, given a handout. Your money, which earlier was income, has taken off into different flows which we will gradually identify. Are you, or the receiver, a worker, a capitalist, a pensioner? It doesn't matter to our analysis. What matters is that we specify accurately the flows, the circulations. This specification includes the instants of exchange but it also includes periods of non-exchange, like the state of the money in your possession. When money is quiescent, it may have no particular designation. But it may also, as it were, be poised for a definite flow. In that sense, in demand function on one level, poised, say, for final basic payment.

The flows of the two classes of payments that we have identified as final payments can very evidently be named flows of expenditure, E' meeting basic goods or services at a certain rate, E'' meeting surplus goods or services at a certain rate. All the rates may be considered to refer to a standard interval of time, selected according to the needs of the analysis: a week, a quarter, whatever. These flows of expenditure are identically flows of receipts by basic and surplus business: we can label them R' and R'' respectively. And here I bring you back, perhaps irritatingly, to the issue of *anonymity*. I typed *business*, not *businesses*. Why? Because, for instance, both basic and surplus business may be carried on by any particular business. Something to chew on there. Now let us consider the flow of initial payments, designated here, with the same convention, as O' and O''. Like E, the flow O has another face: it is income, I, the outlay as received by any factor (or actor) of production. There is evidently no difficulty in writing here that $O = I$. Nor is there any problem in writing $O' + O'' = I' + I''$.

But it would be quite erroneous to break that identity into the two following equations: $O' = I'$, $O'' = I''$. You should pause over this. It is not too difficult to think out, even without our anonymity condition. You simply need to advert to the content of outlay on either the basic or the surplus level. There are wages, there are capital replacements: wage-earners, then, and capital-replacers. So, the outlay has to go at least two ways. But you will have to watch where it goes on *to*. It is altogether better here, of course, if you can persist in thinking functionally, with anonymity and flexibility in mind. Possessors, possessions, poises, of income are the result of outlay. Whether the income is large or small, derived from basic outlay or surplus outlay, a portion of the possessed outlay-income of any possessor is moved by that possessor into the function of basic demand. The possessor has to eat. So it becomes basic income. Recall our illustration of the money in your possession. There is, then, a fraction of basic outlay, say G', that becomes surplus income, and there is a fraction of surplus outlay, G'', that becomes basic income.

Surplus income may seem to you a little odder. Above I mentioned a sub-group that keeps the show going, and with a little effort you can depersonalize this group – quite different from the depersonalization of large corporate decisions – to think of the function of keeping the show going. Who keeps the show going? Who are the capital-replacers? Could it be you, with your few dollars deposit? "It was much harder now to trace the money from beginning to end – from the small saver leaving a few dollars in his local bank to the billion-dollar Eurodollar loans raised by a syndicate of two hundred banks to finance a country in the Far East."[8] The quotation clearly pulls in the larger context of international redistribution and new investment, but our point is the nature of the tracing, which here is by function. And we are trying to build up that tracing by easy stages. You have an illustration of that easy stage in

8 *Sampson*, 190.

88

the purchase of a needed last for a shoe-making business. It is this sort of illustration that fits easiest into the first diagram that we are pushing towards. It may be the case that none of the money in your pocket goes to capital replacing, but you can ponder over the aggregate of pockets and come to appreciate how outlay, basic or surplus, fractions. We already designated the fractions. If $G'O'$ goes to surplus demand function, obviously $(1 - G')O'$ goes to basic demand function; Similarly, O'' splits into $G''O''$ going to basic demand function and $(1 - G'')O''$ going to surplus demand function. So we have $I' = (1 - G')O' + G''O''$ and

$$I'' = G'O' + (1 - G'')O''.$$

Our elementary illustration of your disposal of your pocket-money leaves you, I hope, straining beyond this, raising the question of redistributed money. But it is worth pausing over what we have by means of the following diagram.

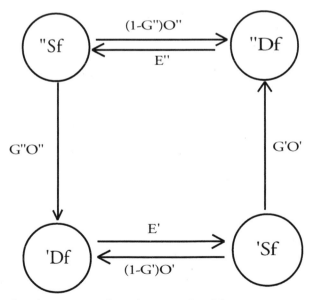

This diagram needs to be completed by a zone representing redistributional activities, but it is thus helpful to us, for you, in making an enlightening comparison with a simple model of economic activity developed by Robinson & Eatwell.[9] No diagram is provided in their text: what I wish to do is develop a diagram from their model that will parallel our own incomplete diagram above. In the model there are two sectors, a corn sector and a machine sector. There are wages in each sector, corn wages, cW and mW – the terminology is obvious. There are profits, cP and mP, and in each case portions of the profits are consumed, eaten, by the non-workers. Again, the terminology is self-explanatory. cPe and mPe are the eaten portions, and the remainders, cPs and mPs, are saved. I am skipping past the various assumptions regarding uniformity, absence of replacements, etc., etc., etc. If you are used to the model business, you find that normal; if you are not, then you find it quite bizarre. The main final point necessary to arrive at a diagram that resembles the above is to accept that what is saved is put back into the process. From this we can get a diagram equivalent to the diagram on page 89.

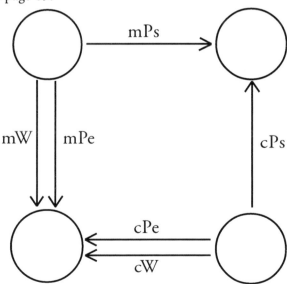

9 Robionson & Eatwell, 89ff.

Absent from this diagram are the equivalents of E' and E'': consumption is of corn received in this organized economy, so expenditure is unnecessary. But otherwise, because of the differentiation of the two sectors, there are clear similarities, and they are worth your following them up. In so far as you do follow them up, and especially if you have the text to hand, you will gradually find deeply- rooted dissimilarities. Even without the text you can make a start by returning to the comments on *An Introduction to Modern Economics* that are to be found in chapter one above, following footnote 16. It is not just the absence of functional distinctions, which is found, for example, in 'consumption of workers and capitalists', mWe + mPe, as compared with our G''O''. It is the entire mentality, the fixity of the descriptive and modeling mentality as opposed to the explanatory and normative perspective at which we aim. We could easily get lost in a detailed discussion: I wish to avoid this, as also to avoid getting you thinking in terms of profit, etc. Still, a single lengthy quotation will give you something to brood over, especially important if the text is not to hand:

> For the economy as a whole, we can look at national income in two ways (i) as the flow of income, and (ii) as the value of expenditure. Thus:
>
> | *Income* | *Expenditure* |
> |----------|---------------|
> | Profits | Investment in machines |
> | Wages | Rentier consumption of corn |
> | | Workers' consumption of corn |
>
> Since workers consume all their wages, it follows that:
> Profits = Investment + Rentier consumption
> What is the significance of this equation? Does it mean that profits in a given period determine capitalists' consumption and investment, or the reverse of this? The answer

to this question depends on which of these items is directly subject to the decisions of capitalists. Now, it is clear that capitalists may decide to consume and to invest more in a given period than in the preceding one, but they cannot decide to earn more. It is, therefore, their investment and consumption decisions which determine profits, and not vice versa.[10]

Let us return now to our incomplete diagram on page 89. To complete it we simply add flows from the redistributive function to the other four functions, S', S'', D', D''.

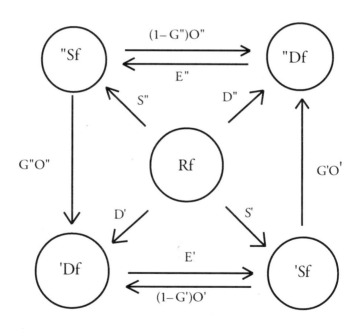

10 Robinson & Eatwell, 95. The reference there is to M. Kalecki, *Selected Essays on the Dynamics of the Capitalist Economy*, Cambridge University Press, 1971, 78-9.

The meanings of the symbols should be evident, and the flows are, as usual, per some defined interval. You must envisage these flows as having all the complexity of concrete business and banking operations, and if you are a beginner in economics this complexity is a pretty vague reality to be tackled in advanced courses. So, S', is a flow per interval to basic supply function, symbolized as read, 'Sf. It goes, of course, both ways: credit given, deposits made, etc. It involves all the varieties of money normally studied, in a preliminary fashion, in elementary texts. It involves also a colourful cutthroat range of activities within the borders of Rf which are not part of our elementary topic: think of the various markets of money, bonds, stocks, takeovers, etc., etc. It involves the distinctions already made between operative payments (e.g. interest payments) and redistributive components in transactions. But do not let all these facets bewilder you at present. S' should have for you now an elementary heuristic meaning: a velocity of money to and from 'Sf. Still, it would be well to bear in mind, as we proceed to talk about money supply, Drucker's cautionary remarks about money and its velocity.

> Take, for instance, Keynes' key theorem: that monetary events – government deficits, interest rates, credit volume and volume of money in circulation – determine demand and with it economic conditions. This assumes – as Keynes himself stressed – that the turnover velocity of money is constant and not capable of being changed over the short term by individuals. Schumpeter pointed out 50 years ago that all evidence negates this assumption. And indeed, whenever tried, Keynesian economic policies, whether in the original Keynesian or in the modified Friedman version, have been defeated by the 'micro-economy' of businesses and individuals, unpredictably and without warning, changing the turnover velocity of money almost overnight.[11]

11 Peter Drucker, "Schumpeter and Keynes", *Forbes*, May 23 1983, 126. See note 30 of chapter one: clearly, a comprehensive heuristic has to anticipate such flexibilities and the ranges of their determinacies and indeterminacies.

We are not trying to handle the micro-economy in this text, but our concrete heuristic theoretic holds to that real flow, and it is best if you can hang on to convenient illustrations as we push along: the butcher, the baker, the candlestick maker in their financial transactions with banks. Note immediately, that unless businesses are expanding or contracting, and allowing for short-term and seasonal fluctuations, the aggregate flows S' and S'' hover around zero. Perhaps the seasonal fluctuation most familiar to you is D' in December?

Our central task in this final third of chapter three is the cluster of problems that pertain to economic acceleration in an isolated economy. Money supply is an evident factor in the problem, so two more terms are needed in our fundamental set: M', the quantity of money added to the basic circuit per interval; M'', the quantity of money added to the surplus interval per interval. The split, I hope, no longer surprises you. Immediately we have

$$M' = S' + D' + G$$
$$M'' = S'' + D'' - G$$

where any of the rates may be positive, zero, or negative, and G is the difference in the crossover to the basic circuit per interval. How are changes in the quantity of money per interval, that are associated with the redistributive function, to be correlated with the transactions of the two circuits and so with the production and changes in production discussed in chapter two? To come to grips with this you have to attend to what might be called sub-circuits of the circuits. We are interested, not in the very indeterminate reality of money changing hands, but in determinable journeys of working money, money operative in the circuits, money that can be correlated with the turnover frequencies of industry and commerce. So we are led to think of, think out, the workings of units of enterprise that supply finished goods or services, units that can be as simple as shoe repairs, as complex as aeroplane manufacture. Here we will stick with our old friend, ploughmaking.

Our island needs about 24 ploughs per year. I am considering here the steady state: a plough culture has been established. Joey has a monopoly on plough-production. She alone produces and sells finished ploughs, but of course she is not alone. Her unit of enterprise, with its various human and material factors, is most likely the complex end unit in a process and even if it reaches from growing trees to storefront it involves, realistically, an interlocking set of contributory enterprises and so various rhythms of transitional payments, etc. But let us keep our focus on Joey's plough turnover. She can meet the annual needs by producing (and selling) 5 ploughs every 75 days or 10 ploughs every 150 days. So there seems no problem: she can sell a plough every 15 days either way, with a suitable seriation of production. But let's get to the nitty gritty of her business.

Such are the structures of her productive process that she is able to finish a plough in 75 days – I am specifying the first option – and she is able to have 5 ploughs in the making at all times. If she was in the second set-up, she would have 10 ploughs in the making at all times, finishing each in 150 days. And here, unkindly, I leave you with the puzzle: go figure! In both scenarios, the volume of business is the same, but in the first scenario, money moves twice as rapidly as in the second. You will find that you need some diagrammatic messing to reach comfortable clarity. Lonergan's general statement should help to focus that clarity. In my illustration and his,

> the difference between turnover size and turnover frequency has been made with exaggerated clarity. It remains that the same distinction can be made with regard to every entrepreneur in basic or in surplus supply. Each one is performing a certain number of services or contributing to the supply of a certain number of products at once. Such performance or contribution takes a certain amount of time.
> But once this time has elapsed, the entrepreneur proceeds to a new batch of services or products. Thus entrepreneurial

activities fall into a series of repeated routines. Further, each of these routines form financial unities: receipts come in for the goods or services supplied; transitional payments are made to other entrepreneurs for their contribution to the supply; initial payments are made to immediate factors; and the aggregate of transactions regarding that batch of goods or services is closed. Thus, the production period has its correlative in the monetary order, namely, the turnover period; and similarly the value of the goods processed or the services rendered in the production period has its monetary correlative in turnover size.[12]

Note that the turnover period is not regularly identical with the production period: the turnover period includes the period of production and sale. Notice further that innovations in payment structures –think of shifts in *plastic* payments – may change turnover periods quite significantly. But these are complications we must pass over in our basic introduction.

The main point to notice is that, in general, a unit of enterprise starts with an estimate of demand – in our case, about 24 ploughs per year – then settles for a more rapid rather than a less rapid turnover frequency: in our case, the option of 5 ploughs in production, one completed every 15 days. That settles the turnover magnitude. Does the need for rapid turnover frequency still puzzle you? It's as simple as the old saying, time is money. In any economy there will be genuinely odd exceptions to this norm: the eccentric who hates to part with a polished and cherished plough or guitar – but in the main the entire economy follows the norm. In doing so, it excludes one possibility of economic acceleration: an acceleration based on a general reduction of turnover frequency. Such an accel-

12 *CWL 15*, section 15; *CWL 21*, chapter 17, section 9.

eration could occur without a change in the quantity of money operating in the circuits, but it is not a realistic expectation.

Clearly, turnover frequency is not inelastic. Brisk selling or lagging sales are intrinsic to its flexibility. Nor is the production period a fixture: it can be varied – even massively, as in shift work, as in war emergencies – to suit demand. But what we are viewing here is a deepening acceleration, a general shift in ideas that generates something beyond short-run and random changes in enterprises, something that involves series and clusters of fresh enterprises. That type of adjustment calls for an increase of money to circulate: more precisely, aggregate increments in monetary circulating capital.

A range of difficulties can occur to you at this stage, especially if you are versed in the strategies of Keynesians or Friedman, or share common clouded notions: that investments equal savings; that interest rates call the play; that retained earnings are key; that gold grounds confidence; that government is mother of progress. We try to steer our way here through present clouds by staying with our island. "Money has well been called the promise men live by."[13] In our island tavern there emerged a promising idea in a context of trust, and it is, literally, given credit. Not *it*, but Joey. The tavern is not a parliament, and there is no reserve of gold or retained earnings, yet there is a structure that we associate with the Italian word for bench.[14] Moreover, the structure of the island's exchange economy is, I would claim, the structure heuristically delineated in our diagram on page 92 : a structure that, so to speak, gives the measure of economies whether in Atlantis or Asia.

We are back with Joey now, not in the steady state of 24 ploughs per year, but in a promising state with no ploughs. You can brood over the promise, trust, credit, as an island ethos centred on a positive S'' in the economy, in our diagram. *Centred on* but much more than that, and the *much more* is something that requires a great deal

---

13 R.L. Heilbroner, *The Economic Problem*, New Jersey, 1972, 352.
14 There is a general introductory discussion of money in *CWL 21*, chapter 3.

of insightful imaging but also what I would call *Rostow reading*.[15] This I must leave to your leisured interest. As you envisage the economic surge on the island due primarily to positive S", you will note troublesome complexities. Nowhere in this little work am I attempting to deal technically with prices[16], but your common notion of an exchange economy will lead you to suspect difficulties related to price fluctuations. Our island economy grows busier as the new credit flows in the economic body like a series of blood transfusions, though there is not just one circulation. There is a lift in employment, a lift in basic income, but as yet there are no extra or new consumer goods and, rather obviously, there is no related call for consumer credit, etc., etc. Let us try for an initial glimpse of the stages from the tavern idea to the stable plough economy, expressing that surge and its problems in a general way so as to leave us capable of exploiting its heuristic openness, each drawing on illustrations available to us in our own cultures, in our own histories.

From chapters one and two you may already anticipate the stages of a major surge and the financial needs that are to be associated with them. The surge begins fully when there is a surplus acceleration; it ends with a basic acceleration; in between there has to be a transition stage. This, in fact, is not a bad start towards a heuristic view of surges. Joey starts the ploughmaking business; in a couple of years ploughs move into agricultural use in a transitional stage; the surplus surge levels off as crop quantity and quality etc emerge from a basic expansion. Nor is it difficult to reach a view of the financial needs. The surplus expansion calls for an increase, indeed an increasing increase, of money in the surplus circuit; the

15 The works of WW Rostow, some of which I cite in the text, represent struggles with the historical data, especially regarding innovations. With such work we associate the names of Juglar, Marx, Schumpeter. Venturing into detail here is worthwhile, although the available literature is within a flawed perspective: see, e.g. FM Scherer, *Innovation and Growth: Schumpeterian Perspectives*, MIT Press, 1984.
16 See note 3 above.

basic expansion calls for an increase in money in the basic circuit. The transition stage is somehow just that: a steadying of surplus financial needs, a surge in basic financial needs.

This simple view should not be too elusive. The monetary needs of surplus acceleration have already been touched on. What of the third stage, the basic expansion? More and more varied goods and services are appearing at the basic final market. Without an increasing increase in basic income, prices would be forced down: a detailed analysis of the dynamics of that effect would bring out its rhythms,[17] but here I am hoping only for a first impression of the key problem of the modern economy. That problem is the cut-off of the basic expansion due primarily to the discouragement, for basic businesses, of shrinking prices. Basic outlay, basic income, basic receipts should keep pace, a climbing pace, with a climbing basic production. But that keeping-pace has conditions which are impossible to fulfil with the present mindset of business and economics. Why this is so will occupy us later.

Meantime, you should pause imaginatively over the gist of our elementary viewpoint, using the fundamental diagram on page 92. We are trying to envisage the financial adjustments to a major surge of the productive process. In a stationary economy, one without innovation or development, the crossovers balance when allowances are made for seasonal and other minor fluctuations. In that state, the crossovers are, of course, constant. But in a surge the crossovers vary, and the problem of macrodynamic equilibrium is that the crossovers must remain dynamically balanced. If they do not remain so, then one circuit is being drained in a way that might seem to benefit the other.

Recall here the illustration, above, of more basic goods and services with no increase of basic income to meet them. Now add a sort of reverse illustration from the surplus expansion: here you

17 See *CWL 15*, section 28; *CWL 21*, chapter 18, section 15.

will notice once again the need for creative imagination, the need to work towards reading the fundamental diagram with as much concrete intention as you can muster. We are not studying mathematics: we are struggling to understand the norms of progress of communities. So, what does G"O" represent as the island moves into the plough business? It represents an interval-by-interval increase in basic income. There is the evident increasing of employment, and the less evident increase of basic income available to all, due to the surplus expansion. Surplus outlay is surging, making possible an increase in basic income: but that increase has, would have, no new flow of goods and services to meet it. Can the possibility be reduced to a mere possibility by some balancing strategy, so that basic prices do not climb?

So much for the elementary indication of the problem of economic surging. I cannot go much beyond it without creating the illusion of summary comprehensibility.[18] We are at the core of Lonergan's revolution in economic dynamics. His own treatment is already stark, summary: what is needed is a 500 page text. What seems to me appropriate here is to mesh hints, concrete allusions and quotations in a manner that will encourage slivers of insight, a sluing of orientation, a slew of interested beginners among which there will eventually be writers of 500 page texts.

First I must encourage you to enlarge, by creative concretion, the elementary view of a clear three-stage surge. Joey just can't start making ploughs: there are no plough factories; machine tools are of a previous idea; etc. All there is is the presence of innovative encouragement. Depending on the character – openness, incompleteness, versatility – of the innovating idea, the steady-state use of capacity in both basic and surplus industries, the skills of the employed and the unemployed, various forms of lift can occur to the economy as it stands. So one can envisage a minor expansion, proportionately basic and surplus, somehow climbing with old implements towards the ramified realities of the new idea. And these expansions generate

18 I have discussed the problem of summary presentation in "Systematics, Communications, Actual Contexts", *Boston Workshop*, Vol. 6, ed. FE Lawrence, Scholars Press, 1986, especially page 147, where I recall Fichte's effort at a "Sun-Clear Statement" of Kant's views, and DeQuincey's treatment of Ricardo's economics.

their own financial problems. *Rostow-reading* is obviously relevant here, but always with the edge of our distinctions. To keep you tuned to that cutting edge I have avoided standard economic terminology – savings, profits, investments, effective demand, national product, whatever – and will continue to do so.

Let me return, then, to the fundamental distinctions of incomes: basic income and surplus income. As I noted at the beginning of chapter one, the word *surplus* troubles me, but I have stuck with it to avoid changing Lonergan's usage. What is surplus income? In a static state it is the income that meets the productive needs of maintenance and replacement: it is, if I might pun a little, *superfluens*, flowing above, but not superfluous, somehow extra or spare. Further, it is no harm to recall that it is a functional distinction: outlay goes to income at all levels of society and it is divided by the community – think of pension funds as well as portfolios – to become either basic or *superfluens*. This division, and the balance of crossovers, is relatively unproblematic in the static economy of a sane society. My use of the word *sane*, of course, indicates that it may well be problematic: there are innovations, financial and productional, based on no ideas, warped ideas, the mongering of ideas of war and welfare, the massive presence of sick ideas of success. These insanities point beyond our present effort. That effort, if it was to have a single focus, could be identified as an effort to call attention to a wrinkle in surplus income, a type of that income that may be called pure surplus income.[19]

19 The interested reader could enlarge greatly on my meaning of the word *pure* by following up the meaning of *the pure desire to know* and the *notion of value* in B. Lonergan's *Insight* and *Method in Theology*. More proximately, there is the implicit notion of a social surplus. Alfred Eichner, in a discussion of the systems approach to economics ("A Look Ahead", *A Guide to Post-Keynesian Economics*, Sharpe, NY, 1979), remarks "Under the systems approach, economics is no longer the study of how scarce resources are allocated. It is instead the study of how an economic system - defined as the set of social institutions responsible for meeting the material needs of society's members - is able to expand output over time by producing and distributing a social surplus"(171). Later he adds "...this means that a consensus must be reached, through the appropriate representative bodies, about the principles which will govern the apportionment of any social surplus"(176). The reader will find it worthwhile to figure out how the present approach sublates both the systems perspective and the characterization of the consensus.

Let us get back to Joey in the tavern and her massively good idea.[20] The idea occurs, normatively, in a context of community, indeed, global concern. It is worth investing in. It is worth the community's while to invest in it. Here I ask you, patient reader, to hang on to our functional distinctions so as to keep a focus beyond Joey. Joey, her banker, the local leather-worker, etc., happen to be at the centre of this ferment. But the ferment is part of the flow of progress that can lead to a lift of life in community and history. And the key to that lift is a shift of surplus income to include the abnormal component that I have named *pure*.

What do I mean by *abnormal*? In a static economy there is normal income. It divides functionally into basic and surplus income: you are used to this distinction by now. One can indeed designate, with heuristic if not concrete accuracy, the spread of both incomes across the community, even around the globe. And however nice an ideal socialist world might seem, normal income is not egalitarian, nor is the proportion of each *normal income* that is surplus democratic. The pensioner's income is small and primarily basic; the bank president's income is considerable and, most likely, primarily surplus.

You may need to pause over this. I am talking about a static economy. What can be meant by *primarily surplus*? The banker has a certain lifestyle with a basic expenditure well above that of the pensioner. The rest of his income, the greater part on my supposition, is primarily surplus in that, in the static economy, it goes to meet the demands of replacement and maintenance. It does so, of course, not directly, but through redistributive operations. What, then, is

20 There seems no harm, at this halfway mark and highpoint of our struggle, in intimating the extraordinary horizon-shifts involved in grasping the meaning of the fostering, identification and implementation, of 'good ideas'. It is the challenge implicit in note 26 of chapter 2 and the quotation there from Lonergan. The final chapter of a forthcoming volume seeks to add further pointers: 'Pure Surplus Incomes, Pure Formulations, Pure Desires", chapter 7 of McShane, *The Redress of Poise*.

pure surplus income? It is not normal, in the sense that it does not belong in a static economy. It is most neatly described as the financial counterpart of new fixed investment, and may be identified in your mind with aggregate savings, though I have been trying to avoid the topic of savings.[21] And now, even if we are not going to develop its financial equivalent, you would do well to recall the analysis of the conclusion of chapter two. New fixed investment – include, if you wish fuller concreteness, the phasing out of the obsolete – is quantitatively rhythmic, with price rhythms regularly in tandem.[22] While we skip here the necessary analysis, you have sufficient sense of the stages of a major economic surge to appreciate descriptively the financial need of an increasing, and an increasing rate, of pure surplus income, as the take-off mounts. Various maxima of average and aggregate pure surplus income will occur as the economy shifts to the basic expansion:[23] I am speaking normatively, of course, in the sense of a financial keeping-pace with the due accelerations of production. Finally, pure surplus income reverts to zero: it, and its production counterpart, has been absorbed into the static state of a higher level of life and money-flow.

We glimpsed already problems associated with the rhythms of what I call pure surplus income. The financial surge, so to speak, does not automatically follow the productive needs: early increases in the wage bill at lower income levels belong normatively in surplus flow; later surplus investment tendencies cut against normative basic needs. Lonergan's blunt comments of 1944 are certainly worth including at this stage. They are not dated.

> Now it is true that our culture cannot be accused of mis-
> taken ideas on pure surplus income as it has been defined

---

21 The topic is treated scatteredly in *CWL* 15 and *CWL* 21: see the index under *savings, Kalecki*.
22 Again, this topic would carry us into deep water. See notes 3 and 17 above.
23 *CWL* 15, section 23; *CWL* 21, chapter 18, section 14.

in this essay; for on that precise topic it has no ideas whatever… net aggregate savings vary with new fixed investment, and the complaint is that there exist, in the mentality of our culture, no ideas, and in the procedures of our economies, no mechanisms, directed to smoothly and equitably bring about the reversal of net aggregate savings to zero as the basic expansion proceeds. Just as there is an anti-egalitarian shift in the surplus expansion, so also there is an egalitarian shift in the distribution in the basic expansion. But while we can effect the anti-egalitarian shift with some measure of success, in fact the egalitarian shift is achieved only through the contractions, the liquidations, the blind stresses and strains of a prolonged depression.[24]

As I struggled to bring this chapter to a conclusion a host of related topics seem to cry out for inclusion: profit and interest rates, monopoly and competition, unions and prices, employment and inflation, war and welfare, law and economics, upper and lower level fixed incomes. Their cry in fact will be heard: the second half of chapter five will place their discussion in a more adequate context, and the epilogue will give further pointers. But it seemed to me best to come to a halt with your focus on the missing idea. As it happened, my concluding coincided with my beginning John Kenneth Galbraith's recent book, *A Journey Through Economic Time*, and I found the point of my halt well articulated in his introduction. "Detail can disguise the hard and essential core. It can also discourage as well as distract the reader."[25]

So I am led to conclude abruptly. My interest is this essay is in generating the missing idea, "to introduce to a patch of ground a

24 *CWL 15*, section 27; *CWL 21*, chapter 18, section 14.
25 J.K. Galbraith, *A Journey Through Economic Time*, Houghton Mifflin Co., New York, 1994, xii. I will return to Galbraith's book in note 37 of chapter 5, indicating briefly there also how the problems listed above - interest rate, etc – are recontextualized by the strategy of functional specialization.

plant that did not previously exist,"[26] but I have no short-term optimism about that generation much less that the plant 'suddenly thrives and overruns it',[27] where *it* is the establishment of economic theory and economic practice, the necrophiliac ills of the twentieth century, the western follies of progress and success. Grasping and elaborating how the idea might effect *it* and *its* ideas pivots on the present slow growth of the idea, the hard and essential core, in you.

So I leave you to ponder about Joey's island as it moves, so unrealistically, to the new prosperities of the plough culture. And, just as unrealistically but profitably, you may now go on to reflect on Joey's daughter, as she stands on the shore one evening and sees a strange canoe approaching, and an idea bubbles from her creative imagination. 'Wouldn't it be nice to share our ploughs with these folk? But we would need something larger than a canoe... '

26 See the frontispiece of the present book.
27 *Ibid.*

Government *&* Globe

The present topic is probably the most manifest to you, even if you are only a beginner in economics. Government taxation clutches at your earning and spending. The media tune you into trade agreements and third world debts. Yet to get beyond the manifest to what is the heart of the matter and the mess is not easy. Economic journals are contemporarily cluttered with erudite articles on taxation structures, fluctuations of exchange rates, export policies of less developed countries, the international debt problem. Our introductory efforts here cannot reach into these subtleties, but perhaps by the end of some serious work on this chapter you will have an angle, the beginnings of a perspective, on missing components of contemporary searchings in the economics of international trade and government operations.

You already have a line on what is missing through your elementary glimpse of the two flows in the economy brought together by our basic diagramming of flows and crossovers. Present economics does not have, much less grow round, these distinctions. The basic and surplus circuits and the requirements for their balanced twining are not a topic in first year university texts, and the absence carries the students forward into the staleness, disorientation, and relative irrelevance of present economic theorizing and advising on trading and taxing. So what we add here to the view of the previous chapters will not resemble regular treatments of these topics. To the precision of our diagram of circuits we will add, superpose, circuits that correspond to operations of international trade and national government. But further, to deal with international economics, we must add diagram to diagram, where each diagram corresponds to what is accepted as an economic unit, a nation or group of nations.[1] Bernard Lonergan, in his first effort to handle this topic, wrote:

> Whether from mental fatigue or from objective impossibility, I do not see that a general study of the inter-action of several mechanical structures is possible. The problems are far too complex. However, what is possible is the solutions of particular issues. Then a definite and limited objective is assigned the inquirer and, as these issues arise, he can prescind from an infinity of irrelevancies to track down the precise point at hand.[2]

We have a limited objective here: to track down in a broad manner the effects of trade and government on the rhythms of the two circuits. The key to the necessary enlargement of our discussion, of getting beyond considerations of a closed economy, is to link economies through their redistributive functions. It may help, initially, to imagine our island thus linked up to the rest of the globe as a unit: so you will have two diagrams of circuits. If your imagination is up to it you can go further to link the world's economic units in layers, like old-style records, with each circuit diagram linked with others only through a central funnel. Let us venture into the topic of a favourable balance of foreign trade in surplus goods and services. We will consider it to be a steady flow, of the same character as

1 Jane Jacobs, *Cities and the Wealth of Nations*, Random House, New York, is helpful here on the problem of economic units and local autonomies. Also useful is Robinson and Eatwell on the question "Why is there a problem of the balance of payments for the UK but not for the county of Oxfordshire?" (245).
2 *CWL 21*, chapter 6, section 46. It was not, of course, a matter of fatigue: economic process is multiply non-systematic. See Lonergan, *Insight*, the index under *non-systematic*.

the other flows in our diagram: let us say, Z" per interval. To reach for the fundamental insights here we slide past concrete complications of exchange rates, lags, multipliers, whatever. I must appeal to you, especially to professional economists, to tolerate this sliding. For instance, my considerations of government operations could well call up questions like 'What of the balanced-budget multiplier?' Such questions are legitimate advanced questions. We are in the foothills, and this is perhaps best brought out by our sticking with simple extensions of the illustrations from chapter one. So here, think of ploughs as being the export surplus good from our island. It will not be too difficult for you, later, to shift to the problem of the export of agribusiness capital goods from that small island off the coast of China, North America, to lesser developed islands.[3]

The ploughs, obviously, are purchased by exporters. For a start think of these exporters as *availing somehow* of the redistribution function to add to surplus demand. The *availing somehow* may seem mysterious to you. Think of it as a problem to be dealt with in a second year university course in finance. It is a matter of financial market operations in short-term loans or long-terms securities regarding the establishment of a foreign debt or the cancellation of a domestic debt abroad.

So, let us focus on Z". We will presently diagram its flow in the circuit, but it is best for you to work, as we go along, towards your own diagrams. To the final diagram of chapter three, then, there must be added a flow per interval, Z", from the redistribution function to the surplus demand function. It then joins with E" to give a total surplus demand of E" + Z".

What is concretely going on must be figured out slowly. From chapter three you have brought some appreciation of the manner in

3 "The habitable dry land surface of the biosphere consists of a single continent, Asia, together with its peninsulas and off-shore islands... the three largest of Asia's off-shore islands are Africa and the two Americas." Arnold Toynbee, *Mankind and Mother Earth*, Oxford University Press, 1976, 32.

which E" and $(1 - G")O"$ may surge, etc. But for the moment maintain a focus on Z". Remember that, in our simple case, the Z" itself is not a surge: it is a flow per interval which may well be thought of as continuing for colonial decades. We may think, then, of a steady level of plough production per interval, beyond the domestic requirements of maintenance, replacement, expansion. The *beyond* is, as it were, called out of the local economy by Z". But called in what way?

Focus on the surplus demand, E" + Z". E" is a continuation of a circular flow – let's not fuss over crossovers here. It comes from outlay and goes to meet outlay, $(1 - G')O"$. For initial simplicity, think of a double steadiness. A plough culture has been established; a plough exporting is also established. Numbers help the inquiring imagination: the economy is producing steadily 110 ploughs, of which 10 are exported. The trick is to notice that the steady state of the economy is peculiar. It is not the steady state of a plough-using island economy, even though the production of ploughs is steady at 110 ploughs per interval. It could help to think the situation out historically, through the beginnings of the venture of export moving the production of ploughs from a steady 100 to a steady 110 after several intervals. But we are thinking here of the situation beyond that surge. The present E" and a corresponding rhythm of outlay are sufficient to keep the higher number of ploughs in production. So now, what of the additional Z" in the next interval? What you must home in on is, indeed, the fact that it is additional, not needed, in a way that should remind you of the discussion of pure surplus income near the end of chapter three. So, within the concrete complexity of the effects of the entry of Z" into the circuits, you can recognize its central reality as a surplus income that is the possibility of new fixed investment. Z" can move to take its place in the redistributive function as that possibility: an unspecified possibility that, of course, need have nothing to do with the production of additional ploughs or new types of ploughs.

Before considering further the circulation of Z'', let us add the same type of favourable balance on the basic level. Instead of the export of ploughs we now consider the export of bananas: it may bring to mind not only the phrase *banana republic* but also the *banana war* of 1994 in Europe.[4] Now we have the export of y bananas per interval, with the corresponding movement of Z' into the economy. We now have E' + Z' as basic demand reaching basic supply and you can recognize Z' as being other than a normal component of the production circulation, as a surplus that is the possibility of new unspecified investment. Let us view all this with the help of our fundamental diagram.

4 The *banana war* in Europe has colonial roots, for example, the British encouragement of banana farming in the Caribbean colonies. In 1994 the British wished to protect, through tariffs and quotas, those loyal sources from South American producers. The Germans, with no such colonies and an 8 kg per person per year appetite for bananas, were for a free market. Also on the side of the free market, of course, were the giant producers Chequita, Dole and Del Monte, with 60% of the world output. In the 1994 battle, Dame Eugenia Charles, the Prime Minister of Dominica, warned that if islanders couldn't make a living on bananas, they might take up cocaine-production.

It is no harm to remind you, even at this stage, that the diagram is an aid to separating and understanding functions. The circles are not places, nor are they, say, groups of capitalist, workers, bankers, exporters. Recall your pocket of money in chapter three. It would be a very worthwhile exercise, as a context for the present chapter, to try to figure out *where*, in relation both to the diagram and to local geography, government is, foreign debt is, the island shoreline is, where Eurodollars, OPEC monies, World Bank transactions are. How do Z' and Z'' *really travel*? What, indeed does *travel* mean in the world of E-Cash?

The diagram represents the functional journeys. I have labeled the parts of the journey for convenience of reference. For simplicity I omit some flows that are concomitant: I will add these when dealing with government operations, but you may well like to work at this yourself. We list, then, the added elements of circulation, tagging on parallel flows:

1a)	Z'		1b)	Z''
2a)	E' + Z''		2b)	E'' + Z''
3a)	G'O' + Z'		3b)	(1 − G'')O'' + Z''
4)	Z' + Z''			

We have, then, (1) Z = Z' + Z'' entering demand function, (2) its expenditure, (3) its identification as surplus income which does not 'immediately demand', so it is (4) located in the redistributive function. You must satisfy yourself, as best you can, by thinking through concretely or with illustrations, by envisaging export transactions, that the functional journey makes sense. Why, for instance, does not Z move more directly to the redistributive function?

The result of the favourable balance is that, interval by interval, there is a new credit item in the balance of payments of our island. The Z' + Z'' per interval was once undifferentiatedly associated with gold importing – you may recall the tradition of mercantilism

– but now it is e.g. a rate of foreign lending, or of the payment of a foreign debt, or the interest on it.

Our simple illustrations leave us far from the concrete complexities of the island's economy, but we can move a step closer to such problems by considering the domestic accumulation of credit in relation to simple surges in the island economy. We have envisaged a steady state of production of ploughs or bananas or both, where a definite fraction is for export. If you think this out in terms of the accumulation of credit, you will be led to suspect that the steadiness is doubtful. The credit is a possibility of expansion, an invitation to some new surging in the economy. The new surging, of course, requires an understanding of surging that mediates a balanced emergence of its benefits: we are back to the problems of chapter three. But let us focus on the effect of Z on an island economy that is going through some process of surging. Recall our reflections in chapter one on the rhythms of an emergent plough culture, and the financial rhythms necessary for that emergence discussed in chapter three. Now there is added a steady (let's not fuss over this) flow of pure surplus income. It obviously gives a lift to the economy but it does more than that. The details of the extra effects require a return to the analysis of chapter three. But I focus only on major facets of the effects: the energetic reader can probe e.g. questions of inflationary effects.

So, for example, the increased rate of savings required for a surplus expansion was seen to be a definite problem: the added flow of surplus income eases that problem. But what of the decreased rate of savings that would yield a healthy basic expansion as well as a leveling of the particular surplus surge? It is, I hope, fairly evident that the added flow eases the burden of the decreased rate of savings or rates of losses. But there is a less evident effect. The added flow encourages expansive tendencies that may focus on a prolonged surplus expansion and a dodged basic expansion. The acceleration can focus on an increment in production that sells abroad, so that the need for lowering higher incomes and raising lower incomes is bypassed.

The previous paragraph is a compendious indication of a heuristic attitude which needs enormous filling out. The paradox of that filling out is that it requires its own application to generate precise instances either in history or in planning. The details of the rhythms considered in chapter three have to be brought into play in understanding particular situations. Also, of course, more complex local rhythms have to be brought into focus or anticipated, as well as the complexity that are present because of synchronization of cycles of various groups of economies or even larger development lags in economic structures. It is sufficient in the present effort if you begin to glimpse the necessity and the plausibility of the functional analysis for the understanding and guiding of the globe's economy. In its fullness it should become the basis of the factual, contrafactual and proleptic analysis of the twists and turns of economies in history and of the hopes for global economic development.

However, even if present categories and mindsets are inadequate to the task of homing in adequately on economic history and economic planning, it is still worthwhile to pause over past performances and current trends to at least see the need of the missing perspective.

My reader will have her or his own leads to broader reflection or local illustrations. The reflection or illustrating should have the character of a heightening sense of the need for understanding rather than a yearning for a quick fix. During my work on this chapter I received a letter from a concerned Mexican – it was during the crisis of early 1995 that was *fixed* by the USA bail-out – asking for a solution to Mexico's economic problems from the perspective of the present analysis. My reply was mainly an effort to intimate the need for a massive shift in the understanding of the complex rhythms, history and geography of production, financing and trading. One might think here of the parallel in the complexity of motions in the galaxies, or even in the solar system of planets, satellites, projectiles: to understand and control such a complex, one has to leave behind broad Aristotelian ramblings about natural motions and figure out how the moon moves, how the penny drops.

The Mexican crisis is, perhaps, in the reader's past, but an event that coincided with my writing may help you muse profitably about local and global needs. Today, March 23rd, I read in *Time* magazine (wondrously dated March 27th 1995) of a 'Maestro in the Wings': 'the venerable but much criticized World Bank wins ovations for its versatile new president.' Centre-page is a picture of James Wolfensohn, the new head coach, playing the cello at Carnegie Hall, but of course the versatility includes his 'extraordinary career in financing and public service spanning three continents.' But does he have a fundamental grasp of the normative rhythms of production, finance, trade? Does he appreciate the basis, the bases, or is he set to coach an early form of rounders? Well, that's another story.

The conclusion of the article has a quotation from Robert McNamara, who headed the World Bank from 1968 to 1981: 'The bank needs intellectual leadership with passion, a willingness to defend itself with vigor.' The reference and sentiment lead me back to my memories of McNamara's unenlightened missionary spirit.[5] McNamara was *parachuted into* the world bank in 1968, the same year that Bernard Lonergan corresponded with me regarding the need for economic enlightenment. Lonergan had been lead to correspond with me by his sense of the inadequacy of JB Metz's political theology which he had been reading. Twenty five years later, in a rediscovered text of Lonergan's on economics, I found Lonergan's point made succinctly, equally applicable to McNamara and Metz: "The vast forces of human benevolence can no longer be left to tumble down the Niagara of fine sentiments and noble dreams."[6]

5 Deborah Shaply, *Promise and Power: The Life and Times of Robert McNamara*, Little, Brown and Co., Boston, 1993.
6 *CWL 21*, chapter 3, section 17.

McNamara came from big business and bombers to banking. In 1968, the Bank's annual borrowings were $735 million, the cost to the Pentagon of a few F-111 fighter-bombers, or less than a month's fighting in Vietnam. So McNamara plunged forward, thinking in billions not millions, and it is worth pondering, with the help of a lengthy quotation from Deborah Shaply's biography, over the perspective and direction of his efforts. The quotation also introduces the perspective of Rostow, also worth pondering over in the light of our elementary struggle.

The field of aid had indeed been experiencing 'frustration' and 'failure' when McNamara was parachuted into it in April 1968. The accepted model for how the new countries of Africa, Asia, and Latin America should modernize was based on the presumed lessons of the industrial Revolution and on Western Europe's recovery after World War II. All societies were presumed to go through stages, from subsistence farming to large-scale agriculture, to a bourgeois, small-business phase, to heavy industry. Only in the last stage was enough capital saved and pooled for reinvestment, which could generate more industrial activity and profits; this was the 'takeoff point' at which growth became self-sustaining and the benefits of growth would 'trickle down' to the poor. The text advocating the 'stages of growth' theory was a book of that title, written by Walt Whitman Rostow, who later became Lyndon Johnson's national security adviser and a proponent of bombing. Rostow had been McNamara's nemesis in his last year in office, and now McNamara learned to criticize his theory of economic growth as well.

The World Bank had followed the stages-of-growth philosophy, not because of its intellectual depth, but because it could be used to justify large loans for dams, power plants, industrial activity, telecommunications – in other words, the kind of lending the Bank knew how to do. For much of the 1950s and 1960s, the theory seemed to work: The gross national product of the Third World grew in the 1960s at an average of 5% per year, which slightly exceeded American and European economic growth. But theoretical stages of growth and trickle down were not working, as any visitor to India or Africa could see by the late 1960s. Officials who dealt with the repeated tragic famines in India and Pakistan, and the hectic emergency shipments of wheat from Alberta, Canada, or Kansas to prevent mass starvation, knew that GNP growth can hardly be an accurate measure of progress.[7]

A thesis of this small primer leads to the claim that McNamara lacked the basis of criticizing Rostow, of taking the measure of the state of economic play, of performing as a head coach. To the problem of measured coaching we will turn in chapter five. Here I make the outrageous claim that the basis of serious criticism and construction is lacking in the ruling economic community. Peter Drucker wrote in the eighties, "By now we know, as Schumpeter knew fifty years ago, that every one of the Keynesian answers is the wrong answer."[8] But this *we* does not seem to include the vast majority either of economics professors or economic advisors.[9]

However, we must break off our distractions to get back to our elementary searchings. As I have repeated regularly, the distractions are not really distractions, but aids to the maintenance of our concrete intention, attention: there is nothing abstract about our analysis. So, the transition to our next consideration of our island's

7 Deborah Shaply, *op. cit.*, note 5, 468.
8 Peter Drucker, "Schumpeter and Keynes", *Forbes*, May 23 1983, 125-6.
9 Paul Krugman, *Peddling Prosperity. Economic Sense and Nonsense in an Age of Diminishing Returns*, Norton, New York, 1994, gives a sobering account of recent American strategies.

balance of trade is helped along by recalling McNamara's dealings with Kenneth Kaunda in the mid-seventies.

Instead of ploughs or bananas we have copper. But now we have the added reality of a plunge in copper prices in 1976. In the crisis the Bank did not pull the plug on Kaunda's Zambia: indeed, the bank went on to fund three unsuccessful agricultural projects. What had McNamara, Kaunda, the economic advisors on both sides, 'in mind' throughout all this? Certainly not a view of two flawed circuits of economic activity, with equally flawed superposed circuits. What was happening in Zambia? What is going forward economically as Zambia moves into the new millennium? What might have happened? Without the realistic and normative perspective on the grim game that we are reaching for here, these questions cannot receive coherent answers. As we will point out in the next chapter, the answers of the future will resemble more the layered pondering and planning of good baseball than the alchemical prognostications of present bankers and professors.

Let us return from these healthy distractions, relevant contextualizations, to our elementary analysis. We have considered the favourable balance of trade. We turn now to the problems of the unfavourable balance of trade. We do not have to cover the same ground again: the circuits remain the same, but now we consider the sum $Z = Z' + Z''$ to be in some way negative. And we can keep the same illustrations, but with a change of focus: our attention, if you like, is on the receiving end, an island receiving the imports. A fuller diagram of the circulations will help our reflections: government operations are still omitted.

We stick with our simple illustrations, distinguishing Z' and Z'' clearly in order to get you used to thinking in terms of these functional distinctions. We focus on ploughs and bananas with the implicit assumption that one is purely surplus circuit, the other basic, although ploughs can be ornaments and banana extracts can serve a surplus function. To muddy the waters round our island, of course, you may puzzle over such an import as the automobile: that import demands a massive functional change of perspective if adequate historical and statistical data for cycle analysis are to emerge. But at present, in this elementary introductory book and effort, we stay as simple as possible.

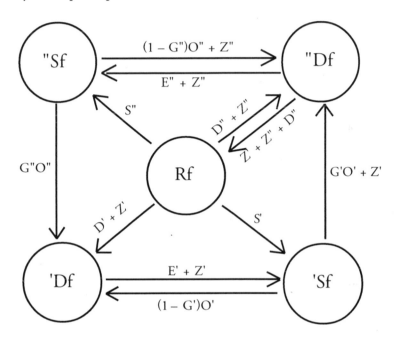

You envisage here, then, that Z' and Z'' are both negative, in the sense that some sort of exporting of finance is occurring. Obviously an unfavourable balance of trade can occur with, for example, a large negative Z'' and a smaller positive Z'. Indeed, some such situation is entirely plausible, for example, in the case of a lesser developed nation reaching for expansion. Such cases call for more refined analysis, pointing beyond our introductory struggle. Finally, we hold to our simplification of a steady rate of Z' and Z''.

While we could carry through our reflections in terms of a negative Z, it is better – easier and also more systematic – to think of the Zs as positive quantities. So, let us focus first on a steady import of ploughs, Z'' per interval, an excess sold on the domestic final market. You have to envisage domestic entrepreneurs directing part of their gross receipts to surplus demand to purchase from the importers the excess imports, ploughs, which are transferred to the surplus final market. In our diagram this is added to the normal circuit flows: 3b: $(1 - G'')O'' + Z''$; 4b: $D'' - Z''$, the redistributive connection. The sale of these ploughs corresponds to an addition to normal surplus sales: 2b: $E'' + Z''$. Notice that the surplus purchasing of ploughs will actually be more than Z'', but such additional costs of domestic production factors – wages, rents, interests, etc. – circulate in the normal fashion. Also, of course, there may be the added complication of incomplete ploughs: they need to be assembled. Again, this domestic complication does not concern us. Z'' corresponds strictly to the surplus import and our focus is on its circulation.

There is no serious problem with Z'' arriving in the redistribution function. The importers use it to pay foreign sellers in some way through the manipulation of foreign debts or securities. The fundamental problem lies with 1b: $D'' + Z''$, the flow of money that is needed to complete the circuit at the other end, that is needed to make the surplus purchase of Z'' per interval. You may have to go back to chapter three to envisage the problems associated with D'', a borrowing per interval for capital equipment. Now we have $D'' + Z''$, which includes an additional *borrowing* of Z'' per interval, for the maintenance, replacement, or net increment of domestic capital equipment. One can, optimistically, envisage Z'' as a 'flow through' from the redistributive function: Z'' is being paid per interval for the excess import, received by those borrowing from abroad or benefiting (through interest or principal) from previous foreign investment or – one thinks of earlier times – selling gold abroad. The optimism consists in regarding all these receivers as willing to funnel their funds towards surplus investment, so giving $D'' + Z''$. But close attention to what Z" is doing will cool any optimism. It is not, like D", purchasing domestically produced surplus goods, the production of which generates a balancing domestic income. What matches the *borrowing* of Z" is a rate of payment for excess surplus income: it is not *calling out*, lifting, domestic surplus activity. That excess may be towards a capital expansion, or it may be merely replacement capital goods. But in either case we have a weak or sick domestic economy, unable either to accelerate itself or, in the second case, to maintain itself. The weakness may be the weakness of a young economy or it may be that of a settled elder. But in neither case is there a scenario of optimistic investment. Domestic investment is unattractive where domestic capital is on foreign crutches. Depending on the age and state of the economy, foreign debts are increasing or foreign holdings are decreasing. A young resource-filled country may surmount the difficulty. But the old creditor country can settle into a chronic condition needing profoundly unattractive measures. Can you survey the globe for instances? The difficulty here is the absence of the functional classifications, basic and surplus, and the rhythmic ramifications. It is like trying to have a clear view on fire-hazardous chemicals prior to the emergence of the perspectives of Lavoisier and Mendeleev.

However, you have reached something analogous to that perspective from our elementary considerations of the previous chapters. It seems late in the day to swing back to the character of those suggested reflections, and to the question of pedagogy and method, but it strikes me as appropriate to do so here. Bad reading habits die hard, and there may be – you may be – the type of reader who simply reads on steadily, not accepting that my words are pointers towards exercises. So let us pause over the messy pedagogical tackling of this balance of trade problem.

What we are doing has its parallel in those elementary experiments of the beginning of learning chemistry: envisaging and discovering simple reactions, verifying simple reaction equations involving hydrogen and oxygen, simple salts and acids. Just as one does not appreciate such reactions through a single demonstration experiment – one can, of course, memorize reaction equations and pass exams quite mindlessly – so here our simple *Gedanken*-experiment has to be supplemented, sustained, enriched, by a serious imaginative effort and endless scribbles. The comings and goings of ploughs, bananas, finances, have to be puzzled about, all the time latched into a struggle with the flow diagrams.

Though the same diagram covers both flows (does this puzzle you, since we seem to have the *wrong sign* on Z in the unfavorable balance?) it is best to work with different diagrams. The two diagrams of favorable and unfavorable surplus trade 'say' different things to you, with a subtlety that depends on how long you work in the conversation! You, many of you, will still find it difficult to think functionally. So, how do you imagine the activities of the flow represented by the lines corresponding to [A] $(1 - G'')O'' + Z''$ *going on to* $-D'' + Z''$ and so on to R? Not, I hope, in terms of suppliers passing money on to buyers who pass money on to some redistributive area.

Eventually your messing may lead you to view the favorable and unfavorable trading as brought out by ordering the flows differently. In the unfavorable trading, the complex flow, [A], just mentioned, can be seen to get the ploughs in. Then a second flow, [B] completes the circuit: $D'' + Z''$ going on to $E'' + Z''$. The favorable trade can be envisaged as reversing these two complex flows. [B] first, getting the ploughs out, then [A] completing the circuit. The same circulation, diagram-wise: can you become clear enough on the shift of reading to talk it out concretely, to teach it? A focus on the redistribution area gives the obvious difference: [B] + [A] leads to accumulation in R; [A] + [B] has the opposite result. And so perhaps you can come to grasp my earlier statement that Z was in some way negative in the unfavorable case?

I am pretty sure that, even with an exercise-laden reading, you are not comfortable with all this. Being really comfortable would mean that you are Basically Adequate, B.A., in economics, and would require perhaps three years messing around in the present perspective. To this topic we will return in the epilogue. The point is best noted here in returning to our analogy with chemistry. Trying to get to grips with the simple reactions of hydrogen and oxygen, nitrogen and chlorine, is difficult, a first effort of chemistry far removed from comfortable control of organic chemistry. Our elementary venture into trade reactions is quite distant from comfortable control of organic economics.

Let us turn our attention now to the problems of excess basic importing. We have the same circuit as we had for excess basic export. No need, I hope, to repeat the pedagogical pointers. The central problem that emerges here is the problem of completing the circuit by something equivalent to consumer borrowing. It cannot, under normal circumstances, be sufficiently met by *dehoarding* and the spending by a rentier class of interest or principal of foreign holdings. Such spending on domestic holdings, of course, is already integral to the domestic circulation.

There is a wide variety of cases of excess basic importing, so let me limit our reflections here to two extreme cases, always within the hypothesis of a fixed Z' per interval. One extreme is that of a necessary excess, the other is what I may call a luxurious excess.

The necessary excess is one easily illustrated by our illustration of banana importing: it envisages the payment of debt, interest or principal, by a banana republic. Our importing island either accepts the bananas, or the case moves into the area of debt forgiveness, repudiation, whatever. You have to think here of a creditor economy gone rentier. There is a past of foreign lending, but now lending does not keep pace with interest and dividends due to former loans, and our banana republic meets its payments with bananas. Now think further of the steady importing in relation to the rhythms of our importing island's economic surges. Suppose the island is in the process of a surplus expansion. Then a failure of the flow 1a is normally all to the good. The actual rate of savings tends to be less than that required for the expansion, and the concomitant excess basic income can be turned to the excess basic import. However, if you put this illustration back into the fuller context of $Z = Z' + Z''$, then the problems of surplus expansion that we noted there will temper a simple optimism about a banana solution.

When the phase of the importing economy is not that of surplus expansion, the failure of 1b, of $D' + Z'$, leans the economy towards depression. The basic monetary flow is not sufficient, at current prices, to meet the flow of goods and services. It is a failure repeated, interval by interval, pushing prices down in the aggregate. Falling prices effect aggregate outlay and income, operations are scaled down, and the fixed Z' becomes increasingly important.

You are, I hope, distracted in your reading of the last paragraph by various facets of the problem, e.g. varieties of price inelasticity, and by possible solutions to it, e.g. government intervention. We are indeed, on the edge of discussing government interventions. But it may be worth your while to go over the paragraph, so to speak, in its primitive simplicity, in a manner closer to the work of chapter one. Then you think, perhaps, of two small Pacific islands with exchange economies related by a debt problem. You need to think it through to grasp clearly the shifting from equilibrium, the shrinkage of prices. Of course, as you think it through, you will arrive at some puzzling about the unnecessary fixity of the amount of money on each island.

Our discussion, however, has been increasingly in a modern context. And the modern context has its evident solutions to the problem: e.g. force the recipients of interest and dividends on foreign holdings to spend their income on the basic final market. The forcing, of course, is done through taxation of those better off; the spending is done through welfare income. To the problem of fixity of money – which disappeared anyway, in fact but not in theory, with the emergence of primitive banking and credit – there is the modern solution of monetary expansion. Such solutions lead us to some concluding elementary reflections on government operations. The other extreme case I mentioned, luxurious excess, is a clear instance of the possibility of such an operation on the economy. Think, for example, of the luxurious excess in the concrete terms of our island moving into a fixed frenzy for strange basic imports: Irish spring water, Russian vodka, pet-dog food (what about food for industrial guard dogs?!) from Australia, the perfumes of Arabia and Paris. The luxurious excess has the same effect as the bananas: but here the government can call, Halt. In the case of the bananas, a halt is not that simple. Not that dealing with luxurious excess is simple, in these days of free trade negotiations.

You may well find the energy and interest to follow up various other possibilities. The most evident other case is had by turning from bananas to that staple of diet and of economic debate, corn, not now needed to handle a foreign debt, and not a luxury, but a basic need. You might well be led into reflections on nineteenth century Britain, and such a broadening is all to the good, provided you hold our focus. What we seek is a grasp of a missing perspective grounded in the classification that emerged from the first chapter. That is what I wish to lead you to seek, whether you turn to nineteenth century Britain or twentieth century Australia, to Keynes' slim reflections on the trade cycle or Friedman's view on money.

The mention of Friedman leads us comfortably back to our topic, the failure of D' + Z' during a steady unfavourable balance of trade in basic goods. Monetary expansion would seem a way to go. But the way of that expansion is not through an insane steady surging of consumer credit. So, one thinks of expansion in terms of increments in entrepreneurial activity: one thinks of (who might this *one* be, thinking in terms of two circuits?!) an S' + Z' or an S" +

Z'. But does this solve the problem? The products of such incre-ments, and they are predominantly capital increments, reaching the final market, are in competition with the excess import. Still, con-traction can be avoided by continued bold monetary policy. The production increments in the surplus market can be bought by sur-plus borrowers. So, this solution to the problem of providing a D' + Z' involves both a D'' + Z' and an S'' + Z'. Interval by interval, there is an increase of debts by 2Z': concretely, of course, Z'' has to be taken into account. But let us think through what is going on in that part of the economic flow which we might designate as Z. Clearly, there is an increase of debt per interval of 2Z'. The Z' to surplus demand can purchase the additional surplus product per interval, and continue circulating to maintain that surplus increment. The Z' to surplus supply function is directed to expand that supply, but its primary achievement is to become the basic income that solves our problem, purchasing the excess basic supply and thus moving back to the redistribution function. The surplus expansion, however, leads to a basic expansion, goods moving to the final basic market, so again the economy is faced with contraction. Unless such basic goods can be moved towards export: that, of course, is the fundamental solution to the problem with which we began.

We have been touching on, but dodging, the operation of gov-ernment right through this problem of the unfavourable balance of trade. Let us now turn our attention to it. Before doing so in our own style, it would be helpful for you to consider a standard el-ementary presentation of the entire topic of our chapter. It is contained in a diagram from the text by Gordon which we have already used. The heading of the diagram might well have been the title of the present chapter: 'Introduction of Taxation, Government Spending and the Foreign Sector to the Circular Flow Diagram'. I include the diagram immediately here.[10]

10 Robert Gordon, *Macroeconomics,* 6th Edition, Harper Collins, New York, 1993, 38.

THE GOVERNMENT SURPLUS OR DEFICIT BALANCES
THE REQUIREMENTS OF THE CAPITAL MARKET AND
THE GOVERNMENT SECTOR

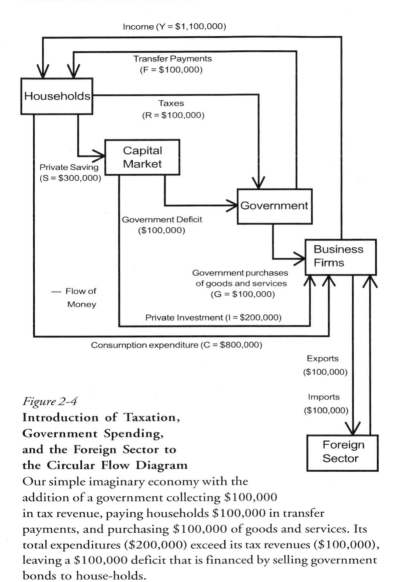

Figure 2-4
**Introduction of Taxation,
Government Spending,
and the Foreign Sector to
the Circular Flow Diagram**
Our simple imaginary economy with the
addition of a government collecting $100,000
in tax revenue, paying households $100,000 in transfer
payments, and purchasing $100,000 of goods and services. Its
total expenditures ($200,000) exceed its tax revenues ($100,000),
leaving a $100,000 deficit that is financed by selling government
bonds to house-holds.

Obviously, it would be a very good exercise for you to try to recast the flows so as to bring this diagram into alignment with our own diagrams as they emerge in this chapter, and it seems best to leave the task to you. The effort will help you to move towards the problems of measurement discussed in the next chapter. But it will also carry you back to the diagrams and discussions of chapters one and three. Most evident is the need for the distinctions that emerged from our first efforts in chapter one. As we saw there, it is not enough to have just households, businesses and a national income. If we are to know what is going on in the economy we need to have estimates, historical, and contemporary and future (in layered tentativity), of the aggregates covered by Y' and Y'', basic and surplus incomes. Y, as given in Gordon's diagram, is simply not sufficient to initiate or sustain an explanatory economics. My reader may well be interested in carrying this criticism forward even to invading the sacred fortress of the unmentionable of note 3 of chapter one. But at least push towards some level of conviction regarding a fundamental need. Simply sketch our baseball diagram and try to locate the elements of Gordon's diagram in it. For one thing, you will reach a healthier respect both for Lonergan's achievement in isolating the redistributive function and for the complexity of that function in national and international economics. Also you will anticipate the need for the distinctions in government operations that we are about to tackle. The problem of taxation and its effects, for instance, require a distinction between surplus and basic taxation that goes beyond vague descriptions of personal and business tax. The problem of government spending likewise must be met by the distinctions introduced below between Z' and Z''. And so on: all this requiring a massive restructuring of historical and statistical inquiry.[11]

11 The distinctions, of course, are not unnoticed or unrecommended. See e.g. Jerzy Osiatynski, *The Collected Works of Michal Kalecki*, Clarendon Press, 1993. In the first essay of the volume, "The Problem of Financing Economic Development", Kalecki writes of sectorized taxation (pages 34, 35, 40). His context echoes

But here we must stick with our introductory effort which may seem little more than impressionistic, even though it does cut through to the essential. The diagram immediately following is the object of our attention for the remainder of the chapter.

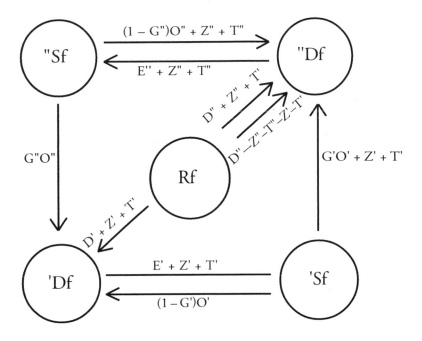

Let us first focus on current government operations without any comment on public debt. Assume steady government spending, interval by interval, of Z' and Z''. This, of course, is the key distinction, making it possible to relate government operations to

the reach of our second chapter: "We shall subdivide the economy into two sectors producing investment goods and consumer goods, respectively. In each sector, we include the production of the respective commodity from the lowest stage. Thus, production of raw materials and fuel will be allocated between the two sectors according to the uses that are made of them in the production of final goods" (23).

the operation of the two circuits, basic and surplus. Without the introduction of this distinction, which we keep noting as necessitating new types of data-identification and organization, we simply do not know what is going on, what damage is being done or undone by government operations. The centre of the economic problem is that there are two circuits: their continuity in macro or micro-expansion or in dynamic equilibrium requires that their normative needs be respected, that their respective outlays and expenditures remain dynamically balanced.

So we turn to the very evident zone of government operation, taxation, and distinguish surplus and basic taxation, T'' and T' respectively, again considered as steady per interval. Now let us consider the case of deficit spending, a case massively verified in the past decades in the locale of my writing, Canada and the United States. Z, then, is greater than T, but this is not very enlightening until we view the circuits. Let us take two sufficiently clear situations: in the first case, Z'' is so much greater than T'' that Z' is less than T'; in the second case, Z'' is so much smaller than T'' that Z' is greater than T'.

Both situations are evidently situations in which one circuit is being drained to the doubtful advantage of the other. If Z'' is greater than T'', then the surplus circuit is being urged to expand, inflate, or settle for redistributional deposits. But a squeeze is put on the basic circuit, so that basic prices are pressured down and basic production is discouraged by this and by the high taxation. The economy is coaxed, interval by interval, towards further surplus activity. The situation may remind my reader of the colonial days, except now such a market may be unavailable.

The other situation, with Z'' less than T'', is one which seems more compatible with welfare tendencies. Surplus income, associated with the rich, is taxed more vigorously, while there is an easing of the tax-burden on the less well-to-do. Z' is then the prime outlet for government spending. Z'' is small and overall surplus activity is discouraged. There is nothing surprising in a resulting consumer price-inflation, in a failure of enterprise, in a decline in both employment and stock value.

You will certainly find it useful to think out other situations, and to extend your reflections to real economies, even though the two flows are not acknowledged with any precision in the literature. But such rambling will help you further towards the significance of the elementary distinctions for the understanding of government operations.

Our two illustrations have been of deficit spending, a regular reality after Keynes, climbing to the North American madness we have already noted, with its consequence in a bewildering burden of debt. The Reagan administration doubled government debt from $1 trillion in 1981 to $2 trillion in 1986, and in that period the United States moved from being the globe's major creditor to being the largest debtor. Of course, when we think of debt and debt-servicing we are likely to focus on the impossible situation of the lesser developed countries, especially the Latin American debt. You may even be familiar with various suggestions regarding solving the debt problem. It is best to use any such familiarity only to bring forward your appreciation of the need for a change to a scientific perspective: otherwise, as I have witnessed, discussion of the relevance of circulation analysis floats towards the floods of erudite commonsense chat.

So, let us make a very general foray into the question of debt servicing, beginning from the diagram of the processes of government spending and taxation. You have noticed already, no doubt, the parallel between such processes and the favourable and unfavourable balances of trade. For that reason, and to conform with Lonergan's usage in his work, I stuck with the variable Z as the superposed variable. You might well find it convenient, in your exercises, to use more precise terminology, e.g. F (foreign) for international trade, P (polity) for government, especially if you are trying for a total diagram. The process of debt-servicing will normally parallel the unfavourable balance of trade. We are not in need of a new diagram: the only difference in this topic is an added focus on taxation, T' and T'', as related to the payment of interest and the provision of amortization. So we have superposed circuits as indicated in the diagram. It is useful to list the components of the total process of government operations:

1) $D' + Z' + T'$ $D'' + Z'' + T''$

2) $E' + Z' + T'$ $E'' + Z'' + T''$

3) $(1 - G')O' + Z' + T'$ $(1 - G'')O'' + Z'' + T''$

4) $D'' - Z' - Z'' - T' - T''$

First let us attend to the circuit of government spending. The deficit spending by government at all levels - federal, provincial or state, municipal – leads evidently to the first two elements, from the redistributive function to demand. The spending, Z' and Z'', shifts a proportion of current production towards public use or even waste - think of rounds of practice ammunition. The income, not spent by individuals targeted by previous outlay, is pure surplus income, which gives elements 3 and 4 on our list. Let us not push further into the possibilities of this surplus income: we may consider it as going to the purchase of government securities. Such purchasing may be seen as curtailing inflation. Of course, one might envisage a perfect taxing system as doing the same thing: but such perfection belongs with the political order of a Plato's kingdom. What we are struggling to see are the consequences of the real mess that economies can move towards, interval by interval. The historical reality of the mess, indeed, is that Z' and Z'' are in no way steady, and even the most election-conscious government has to face the vision of vast rentier class living off the income of government bonds.

So, we have, for example, the problem of enlarging T' and T'', at some crisis stage of the history of an economy, where the public debt has mounted, usually at some irregular rate, with tax in the aggregate less than spending. That public debt may be viewed here as unrelieved by any sinking fund, as being a permanently large sum on which interest is paid.

There are certainly inflationary, revolutionary and capital-levying solutions to the problem, but none of these solutions are associated with confidence in a permanent government. So we must think of the meeting of the issue by massive taxation: T'' and T' per interval to meet amortization and to be paid as interest to rentiers. If such taxation is not to contract the circuits – a topic already touched on in some elementary cases – then the fourth element of the superposed circulation must be matched by an equivalent entry into the circuits. What are the possibilities of such a contribution, T' and T'', to the first element of the superposed circuit? T' would have to be a mixture of rentier standard of living with a lower income boost through dole, social security, or such: the latter boost itself depending on taxation. T'' in element 1 would have to be a rate of investment, balancing the rate of taxation, but still having an accelerating effect in new fixed investment. I will leave you to creatively imagine just how tricky this equivalent entry might be. But granted this first element, the rest follow, carrying forward the inflation of basic income and the flow of surplus income already mentioned.

All this is too hurried and I have no doubt that you find coming to grips with it, indeed with the entire problem of superposed circuits, quite difficult. It needs the 500 page text, with detailed discussion of instances. As I write, the European community are considering a common currency, but one of the Maastricht criteria for joining is a government debt of less than 60% GDP. Only three countries make the grade, Germany, Luxembourg and Ireland: the latter only by slight of hand! Such details, even without our functional distinctions, can help towards entry into the present perspective. One of the benefits of the struggle with them is that it leads you back to chapter three, especially to the problem of the nature and possibilities of pure surplus income. The key benefit is to heighten your suspicion that without the distinction of the basic and surplus activities, one is trapped in relatively ineffective description, unable to detect or anticipate local or global economic performance with any accuracy. Of course, the suspicion is there already in the popular mind, crystallized humorously in the search for a one-handed economist, or in the question, How many economists does it take to put in a light bulb? The heightening, even after four chapters, may be little more than an informed glimpse that Lonergan's suggestion is worth following up. His claim, at the end of his own discussion of superposed circuits, is blunt and simple:

> There exist two distinct circuits, each with its own final market. The equilibrium of the economic process is conditioned by the balance of the two circuits: each must be allowed the possibility of continuity, of basic outlay yielding an equal basic income and surplus outlay yielding an equal surplus income, of basic and surplus income yielding equal basic and surplus expenditure, and of these grounding equivalent basic and surplus outlay. But what cannot be tolerated, much less sustained, is for one circuit to be drained by the other. That is the essence of dynamic disequilibrium.[12]

12 *CWL* 15, sections 29-31. The discussion there of superposed circuits is complemented by other treatments of the topic, available in *CWL* 21. See the index.

A Rolling Stone Gather *Nomos*

You, my patient reader, will, I hope, be quite pleased, as you move into this last chapter, that my final decision regarding its content was to keep it as much as possible concretely and popularly comprehensible. As a beginner, you are not immediately interested either in the theoretical possibility of measurements that relates to the practical exploitation of this analysis or in demonstrations of the impossibility of measuring non-financial capital.[1] You may never have heard of such economists as Walras, Sraffa, Von Neumann, Debreau, much less been lead to suspect the limitations of their perspectives. On the other hand, you have surely some sense of economic advice that does not pan out, of quick fixes by governments, banks, businesses, that fix nothing permanently or even temporarily. My interest here is closer to this sensed need. Our efforts here will be directed towards glimpsing concrete possibilities of arriving at strategic advice regarding communal economic behaviour.

"It may be said in passing that, in the market for strategic advice, the revealed preference of companies is to use management consultants and business-school academics rather than economic theorists. The former group tend to have few, if any, theoretical preconceptions, and draw instead on a wide range of practical experience."[2] The quotation from Ormerod's recent critique of contemporary economic thinking makes a good point, with weaknesses that will help us forward. Let us consider a company seeking coaching:

1 Lonergan deals with the theoretics of measurement in *CWL 15*, sections 17, 23; *CWL 21*, chapter 17, section 11.
2 Paul Ormerod, *The Death of Economics*, Faber and Faber, London, 1994, 57.

Ormerod's point is that the company does not normally seek a coach among the usual representatives of orthodox economics. In chapter four I introduced the notion of coaching in our reflections on World Bank leadership, and now I use the title 'coach' very deliberately: it will serve to bring into focus the main drive of this elementary chapter.

So, let us both think of coaches as we may know them in sports familiar to us. As I admitted earlier, baseball is not my game, but soccer has been for more than fifty years, with twenty years of play, and in more recent decades international tennis. However, as I worked on the difficulties of a transformation of the *game* of international economics, I grew to appreciate the value of developing an analogy from baseball.[3] Still, you may not be a sports-person at all.

---

3 It was, in fact, the reading of Anthony Sampson's book, *The Money Lenders: Bankers and A World in Turmoil*, Viking Press, New York, 1981, which led me to develop an analogy from games. A couple of quotations are useful in the present chapter, as we turn towards international economics. Both quotations refer to Zaire's troubles in the seventies, where loans financed such extravagances as the manufacture of jumbo aircraft, five hundred British double-decker buses, steelworks. By June 1975 Zaire stopped paying interest on most of its debts. One banker described the hustle of bankers in terms of rugby football, when a player loses his pants. "They all go into a scrum to make sure that no one can see... that's how bankers behave when they see a default" (151-2). On the issue of bank rashness, "I asked one of the supervisors, 'is it like a gigantic game of chicken?' 'Yes, you could call it that, but with a lot of other games too. The funny thing about banking is that at the top it's very metaphysical" (214). My use of an analogy from baseball obviously came from the fundamental diagram. Later in my work Professor Michael Shute, researching economics in the Lonergan Archives, found the 1.3 pages from which I quote below at note 14. They confirmed for me the suspicion that I was on the right track. Is, then, a games-theoretic approach relevant? My correspondence with Lonergan in his last years shows his interest in this question. A creative critique of games theoretic economics would carry us very far afield. However, some general flaws in conceptions and applications of probability are discussed in P. McShane, *Randomness, Statistics and Emergence*, Gill and MacMillan, Dublin, 1970, chapters 4 to 8.

Then you must move the analogy to some favourite area: to Pavarotti coaching voices, to Nadia Boulanger, the gentle tyrant of music.[4] The weakness of Ormerod's view is the claim that business consultants have few, if any, theoretical preconceptions. We are back, of course, at a topic that I introduced at the end of chapter one, but I see no way round it. The problem is one of massive disorientation, especially in the universities,[5] regarding what a theory or a theoretic preconception is. The disorientation is rooted in a millennium-long practice in education.[6] And it is worth recalling here Lonergan's conviction regarding the core need of our economic future: "It presupposes a grasp of new ideas. If the ideas are to be above the level of currently successful advertising, a serious education must be undertaken. Finally, coming to grasp what serious education really is and, none the less, coming to accept that challenge constitutes the greatest challenge to the modern economy."[7] Let us take a small step towards appreciating the need and the strategies of meeting it.

Ormerod notes that the business consultants "draw instead on a wide range of practical experience." What does he mean by *draw on*? I recall now a chap that I met on his way to Toronto from Halifax. He had spent only a day in Halifax, *troubleshooting* in a telecommunications business and was returning with a fat fee. He had just "tapped in" to the system and sorted out what, for him, was a minor problem. I joked him about coming all that distance *to tap*: he

---

4 Pavarotti's master classes may be familiar to you; less familiar the strange French genius Boulanger. A convenient biography is Alan Kendall, *The Tender Tyrant. Nadia Boulanger. A Life Devoted to Music.* (with an Introduction by Yehudi Menuhin) Macdonald and James, London, 1976.

5 We are back, of course, in the larger context of notes 4, 7, 17 of chapter one.

6 Oddly, failed practice is not so difficult to recognize. Aquinas put it rather neatly in the thirteenth century, when he described two types of instruction. Roughly, there is an instruction that informs, there is instruction that leads to understanding. The former can leave one certain of facts, whether regarding Pythagoras or Plato, but '*vacuus*': not, then, a troubleshooter or a coach. See *Quodl.*, IV, a.18.

7 *CWL 15*, section 24, conclusion.

joked back, "well, it's knowing where to tap." Obviously, this is the sort of troubleshooter that one would like *not* to have to fly in to handle either national or local economics. I am envisaging here, and invite you to ponder, a distant future, when men and women will be able to *tap in* on local, national and global economic needs, to give history's direction a small or large turn towards adequacy. I envisage such people not only in World Bank and local bank, multinational corporation and corner business, but as a cultured community, *economically literate*. When they emerge they will have *drawn on a wide range of practical experience*, economic successes and failures in history. The strategy of drawing is quaintly indicated in the title, and will be our final topic here: taking the measure, the *nomos*, by a globally-structured cycling, grinding, of human yearning's past. The emergence will be a new order, eventually what Lonergan writes of as a third stage of meaning.

> It will give new hope and vigour to local life and it will undermine the opportunity for peculation corrupting central governments and party politics; it will retire the brain-trust but it will make the practical economist as familiar a professional figure as the doctor, the lawyer or the engineer; it well find a new basis both for finance and for foreign trade. The task will be vast, so vast that only the creative imagination of all individuals in all democracies will be able to construct at once the full conception and the full realization of the new order.[8]

That task, creative imagination *drawing* on the full range of

8 *CWL* 21, chapter 3, section 17.

practical experience, will be our final introductory topic. But the glimpse offered of it depends on our pausing to ask what might you and I mean by *creative imagination drawing on*. The telecommunication expert that I mentioned earlier did it, but did not appreciate what he was doing. This lack of appreciation, and the lack of appreciation of its lack, is the crisis not just of our time but of the next few millennia. The issue here, however, is the crisis of my reader, your patience in homing in on trivial experiences. "In the midst of that vast and profound stirring of human minds which we name the Renaissance, Descartes was convinced that too many people felt it beneath them to direct their efforts to apparently trifling problems."[9]

So, I ask you now to *draw on* yourself, creatively, imaginatively, yet accidentally, to discover why, in the following array, some letters are on top, some below:

> A   EF…
>   BCD…

The dots indicate that I could continue the array to Z. Such continuation might help you. I have had occasion to spend a couple of hours, messing around helpfully, before some particular individual, especially if over-anxious, managed to *draw on* her or his resources to leap to an answer. To *draw on* is to be sufficiently relaxed and interested, uninhibited by any mix of self-doubt and cultural pressure. The achievement is a leap of insight, and usually the laughter of embarrassed relief. But the achievement that I invite you towards here is beyond that: it is the achievement of appreciating the dynamic of that elementary achievement. Further, the significance of that incipient *second-order* achievement is that the dynamic is the same whether the array is simply the ups-and-downs of the alphabet or the more complex and painful ups-and-downs of one's own life or of the economy.

9 B. Lonergan, *Insight*, the beginning of chapter one.

However, if you are to appreciate the quality of a good coach – a second-order achievement – you must pause over a more complex illustration. It is in fact a simple geometric illustration. If you are repulsed by geometry, then you may find it easier to pause over, ponder about, some such pause as looking bewilderedly under the bonnet of your halted car. At any rate, here is my geometric image:

a

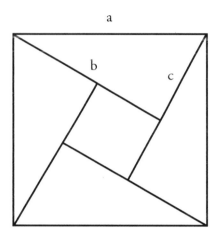

Staring you in the face is Pythagoras' famous theorem: $a^2 = b^2 + c^2$. But it may not be. Recall the telecommunications expert: you may not know how to tap in. Further, *not knowing how* may be a positive reality in you, a disorientating education. The most pertinent illustration of this is the *well-educated* economist trying to tap into this book. What is the missing know-how? It is, simply, the habit of understanding Euclidean geometry up as far as that theorem. The habit, of course, is best recognized by its absence: the professor fumbling with notes, the teacher who lacks vibrant illustrations, the student with a stock of rote answers. None of these can coach or troubleshoot.

If you have been struggling with me through the previous chapters, the effort required to get beyond our present two diagrams to some comprehension is not foreign to you. What is novel here is the change of focus, the extra twist in seeking *concrete strategies at arriving at strategic advice* about economic behaviour. But the extra twist points way beyond this elementary book. Still, perhaps you have already a glimpse of the parallel. The good coach in any sport or art has a complex *preconception*, a network of long memories and immediate anticipations. It is the incarnate reality of comfortable understanding that mediates performance in the team or in the tennis player already tuned to collaboration.

You should take time now to oscillate in your reflections on our baseball diagram as it refers to baseball and to economics. There are comparable subtleties of coaching and *playing* in both cases, of keeping the flows of pitching and running *just right*, despite opposition. The opposition in the economic community is not as evident as another team. It is an opposition within each of us between self-regarding stupidity and cosmopolitan care, and this is altogether too large a topic for an elementary concluding chapter.[10] So let us restrict our reflections to some aspects of balancing the flows indicated in the various two-circuit diagrams of the economy.

Perhaps it is best to begin with a touch of optimism. I have to hand bulky printouts from a certain North American bank - obtained discretely, of course. They indicate the solid possibility of moving to refinements of measurements that differentiate flows of the redistribution function to and from the productive circuits. The refinements require the mediation of further precisions of the present analysis coupled with the continued advances of techniques associated with the so-called information highway. An evident illustration of the needed refinement are distinctions of basic and surplus borrowing and saving and credit that are undifferentiated in such industries as transport and power corporations. Moreover, the information highway must be demythologized: it is a source of more

---

10 For an initial grasp of biases – dramatic, individual, group and general – and their role in decay, see B. Lonergan, *Insight*, Chapters 6 and 7.

or less structured data, and the structuring relevant to the emergence of explanatory dynamic economics is a massive creative undertaking.

But that undertaking will be powerfully assisted by developments in the technology of imaging, estimation and communication. Here, I think, one should be positive about the providence of such timely parallel advances. We will gradually, in this chapter and the epilogue, move towards glimpsing a global collaboration: that global collaboration in economics could perhaps be envisaged as calling forth *peace-game*s in economics of much more subtlety and significance than present international war games.

I am inviting you to stretch your creative imagination here to envisage layers of restructuring. There is the restructuring of academic collaboration, to be treated last in this chapter. And there is the more distant fruit of that restructuring, a transformation of democracy.

But that distant goal must start with the elementary breakthrough envisaged in this brief text. If you have been with me sympathetically so far, the need for the breakthrough has become vaguely evident. A massive obstacle is the academic establishment in economics, linked with a general interdisciplinary exclusion of minding and the minding of minding. But time and the continued failure of this ethos is against that establishment, and I would like to think that this reading is becoming a seeding in you of a green movement in the environment of minding, and indeed of minding minding. The seeding reaches for interdisciplinary thinking that is increasingly lucid with regard to its own creativity and commitment. "Is my proposal utopian? It asks merely for an interdisciplinary theory that at first will be denounced as absurd, then will be admitted to be true but obvious and insignificant, and perhaps finally be regarded as so important that its adversaries will claim that they themselves discovered it."[11]

11 B. Lonergan, "Healing and Creating in History", *A Third Collection*, edited by FE Crowe, Paulist Press, New York, 1985, 108.

So, there will come forth. slowly and laboriously, in a new context of minding minding, historical and proleptic estimates of the relevant economic flows and their sub-flows, of P'Q', P''Q'', dP', dQ'', T', Z'', D', S'', etc., etc., etc. Of central significance, of course, will be the estimates of divided outlays as they give rise to fluctuations in the cross-overs, and it is worth adding a little old-style imaging here to help you reflect on the impact of cross-over fluctuations. I reproduce here a table from Lonergan's writings on economics that gives the value of G''/G' for various values of G' and G''. You recall that G' is the proportion of basic outlay that goes to surplus demand function and G'' is the proportion of surplus outlay that goes to basic demand function. The equality of crossover, G'O'' = G''O'', gives rise to the relation G''/G' = O'/O''. Let us table this fraction.

G''＼G'	50%	20%	10%	5%	1%	0.1%
50%	1	2.5	5	10	50	500
80%	1.6	4	8	16	80	800
90%	1.8	4.5	9	18	90	900
95%	1.9	4.75	9.5	19	95	950
99.9%	1.98	4.95	9.9	19.8	99	990
100%	2	5	10	20	100	1000

As the table makes clear, a variation in G' is much more significant than a variation in G''. If G' were 10% and G'' were 90%, then G' moving to 5% would advance the proportion from 9 to 18, but G'' moving to 95% would advance the proportion from 9 to only 9.5. Inversely, when G'' is 90% and G' is really 10% but estimated to be 20% by over-zealous depreciation charges and by depressed wages, then a normative proportion of 9 is given a monetary distribution corresponding to a proportion of 4.5. The result is an over-production or an insufficient purchasing power or a mal-distribution (or whatever it is safe to call it, for superficial economists fancy the thing cannot exist) that generously slices off about half of existing economic activity.[12]

By up-to-date analyses and imaging, our perspective on all the variables and their interconnectedness, nationally and internationally, can be refined so that economic possibilities and probabilities[13] can be anticipated. It is crucial to notice, however, that no matter how precise the estimates of past and present economic flows become, what I call the predictive mentality of contemporary science must be shaken off. The helpful parallel here is again baseball. Modern techniques make it possible to give details of averages, etc, shifting even as games are played: but they do not make possible predictions. Certainly owners, managers, coaches, pitchers, etc. – even punters – do not predict: they anticipated and hope. Economics must become more like baseball, less like Newtonian astronomy. As I struggled to develop the parallel with baseball in far more detail than can be included here, a fragment of Lonergan's work, left aside by him, was brought to my attention that I think you will find helpful. It is not quite a baseball image, but Lonergan views the five bases as zones of exchange of balls where there is a problem of having a proper number of balls on each base. I quote the concluding half of the fragment:

Evidently, there is a high degree of indeterminacy to the

12 *CWL 21*, chapter 4, section 30.
13 I use probabilities here in the technical statistical sense. See note 3, above.

events within such a dynamic structure. All one can say is that the game may go all awry. A large and positive cross-over difference uncompensated by action from the pitcher's box will result sooner or later in depriving the groups at second and third bases of all their balls, or if the cross-over difference is large and negative, it will result in depriving the groups at home and first of all their balls. Similarly if the group at the pitcher's box makes up its mind to accumulate balls, tossing back fewer than they receive, the groups at the bases will again find themselves without balls eventually. But without further information one cannot say how rapidly the ultimate event of being without balls will arrive. Further, the players at the bases may make up, by a greater efficiency in pitching and catching what balls they have, for any loss of balls they may suffer, up to the ultimate moment when they have no balls at all.

But despite this almost baffling indeterminacy, it remains that there is a definite dynamic structure. There are hypotheses on which the game can go awry; and this possibility constitutes a fundamental determinacy for the structure. On that basis either by adding further information about the nature of the game or by adding further suppositions, a still greater determinacy may be built.[14]

For a glimpse of such greater determinacy I would invite interested economists, but hardly beginners, to turn towards various follow-ups on Schumpeter's work, but always with a critical suspicion of the proleptic modelling business towards which some of his followers lean.[15] Ragnar Frish, the earliest modeler of Schumpeter, illustrates diverse tendencies. On the one hand he can write of pumps

---

14 *CWL* 21, chapter 14, section 3.
15 Chapter 3 of Woflgang F Stolper, *J.A. Schumpeter. The Public Life of a Private Man*, Princeton University Press, 1994, gives a survey of the modelling of Schumpeter's view.

and pendulums and rocking horses – an analogy from Wicksell – and so point towards what I would call heuristic closure. On the other hand he can reach towards filling out the basic heuristic: "By assuming reasonable *ballpark* estimates for the magnitudes of his various parameters, he could produce both Juglar and Kitchin cycles. In the article there is no mention of any long wave, but in his lecture notes he did also produce a fifty year cycle."[16] It is worth noting here a parallel in Lonergan's work, a component of it which I considered too complex for my short introduction. It comes from his heuristic analysis of the manner of which cyclic fluctuations of prices occur during a major surge. In it he succeeds in specifying three crises that might be expected to occur during that surge, or as he calls it *cycle*.

> It may be noted that the triple crisis per cycle may perhaps correspond to Professor Schumpeter's combination of three small cycles named Kitchins in one larger cycle named a Juglar which has a ten-year period.[17] The pattern of six Juglars in one sixty-year Kondratieff would seem to result from quasi-logical connection between successive long-term accelerations. A fundamental transformation of the capital equipment of an economy needs preparatory long-term accelerations that open the way for it; and once the fundamental transformation is achieved, there are other subsidiary transformations that for the first time become concrete possibilities. Such a time series has more affinities with a philosophic theory of history than the merely mechanical structures that we have been examining. A theory of the Kondratieff is in terms of the precise nature of the funda-

16 Wolfgang F Stolper, *op.cit*, 70.

17 Joseph Schumpeter, *Business Cycles*, McGraw Hill, New York, 1939, Vol. 1, 170.

mental transformation, e.g. railroads, but the theory of the Juglar and Kitchin that has been developed here depends solely upon the productive process and the measure of human adaptation to the requirements of an acceleration in that structure.[18]

Further suggestions regarding surge analysis, the avoidance of overdeterminations and of course the foolish determination of basic indeterminacies such as the value of capital, the just distribution of income, and legal specifications of economic utility, would be out of place in your beginner's struggle.[19] Perhaps, indeed, it is best to wind towards our final topic, academic collaboration, with a slice of humour borrowed from the historian of economics, Moses Abramovitz. "There is still too much that is poorly understood about the influence of relative factor costs, about the evolution of science and technology, and about the political and economic institutions and modes of organization on which the discovery of new knowledge depends." "Perhaps some of you are thinking 'If we are already

---

18 *CWL 15*, section 28; *CWL 21*, chapter 18, section 15.

19 The debate on the pseudo-problem, the measurement of capital, has generated a vast literature. The discussion of distribution, a genuine problem, continues, but obviously without the normative foundation that emerges from our analysis: a classical presentation is Maurice Dobb, *Theories of Value and Distribution Since Adam Smith*, Cambridge University Press, 1973. A general view of legal aspects of economics is available in *Law and Economics*: 2 Volumes, edited by Jules Coleman and Jeffrey Lange, Dartmouth Publishing Co., England, 1992. Volume 2 brings out the utilitarian entrapment of legal economic thinking. "Many of the doctrines and institutions of the legal system are best understood and explained as efforts to promote the efficient allocation of resources," Richard A Posner, *The Problem of Jurisprudence*, London, 1990, 20-21. For a serious effort to lift the methodology of law out of conceptualism, see Bruce Anderson, *Discovery in Legal Decision-Making*, Kluwer Academic Publishers, Netherlands, 1996.

ignorant of 90% of the sources of *per capita* growth, how much worse can it be? Can it be worse than 100%?' In a sense it can. Remember Mr. Dooley: 'It ain't what we don't know that bothers me so much; its all the things we do know that ain't so.'[20]

To Abramovitz's humour I add the humility of Schumpeter, to give a perspective on the fuller task. "Scientific analysis is not simply a logically consistent process that starts with some primitive notions and then adds to the stock in a straight-line fashion... Rather it is an incessant struggle with creations of our own and our predecessors' minds."[21] The fuller task that I move towards sketching, first in allegory, then in its warsome wearisome demands, will certainly not find an immediate market. My hope is that you, the uncommon Common Reader, will find it plausible and make that plausibility noised abroad. But at all events I take consolation, with

20 Moses Abramovitz, "The Search for the Sources of Growth: Areas of Ignorance, Old and New", *The Journal of Economic History* 53 (1993), 237, 219.

21 Schumpeter, *History of Economic Analysis*, 4. You will, I hope, turn to think here of your own struggle in this or any other context. It is the struggle of creative reading and it occurs in all domains, at all levels of achievement: Karajan struggling to read Beethoven; Turner struggling to read the sea. I recall Lonergan struggling in his late seventies, as intimated to me in some of his letters: his struggle towards a fuller definition of money; his struggle with the elementary misdirections of the 1978 edition of Gordon's text, to which I have regularly referred. On Gordon: "I have learnt a lot on many topics. Most important I now know how my analysis differs from Gordon's and presumably others. He gives as the empirically determined propensity to consume 75% and to save 25%. For me these are variables with saving increasing in the surplus expansion and consumption increasing in the basic" (Letter of January 10, 1979). Another letter (March 21, 1981) reminds us of his continued reading of Schumpeter, *History of Economic Analysis:* "I am finding helpful background for the Post-Keynesians in Schumpeter's *History of Economic Analysis.* Neoclassical 'neutral money' is not from Walras who sharply separates his *numeraire* from *monnaie* (page 1087). He finds the *Tableaux economiques* and the development of marginal analysis to move towards a general equilibrium (918), and I would add that the equilibrium would not be both general and micro once macro is solidly established."

Madelaine L'Engle, in the caption of an old cartoon: "We're sorry Mr Tolstoy, but were not in the market for a war story right now."[22]

So we move to envisage the larger humble global task, and in order to lead you to an introductory glimpse of it I invite you to venture into what might seem an allegorical distraction. Bear with me.

My story is of a Toronto family that has a holiday cottage at some lake north of the city. Your imaginings might best be served by thinking in your own environ of escape from Bombay, escape to a dacha, whatever. Twenty years previously, Molly and Poldy, both in their early twenties, inherited the cottage, and it has been their July holiday spot ever since. At that time their children, Zack and Till, were toddlers of ages 2 and 3 years. Over the initial years the holiday group grew to include Molly's mother, Moses, and Poldy's brother-in-law, Tseng. After twenty years the holiday group is now Grandma Moses, aged 68, Uncle Tseng, aged 50, Molly and Poldy both at 43, Zack at 22 and Till at 23. They regularly pack up and head for the cottage each July. And increasingly over the years the reality is that they are not happy campers.

You may already sense the direction I am taking, and so I repeat my regular appeal for concrete intention and imaging. My classroom leisured discussion always allowed the emergence of personal anecdotes of hidden miseries and pretended joys: an Oscar Wilde could elaborate with a Dorian Earnestness or a Chevy Chase. So, in my version, Grandma Moses' real joy has grown over the years to be bingo: it is left behind during *vacation*. Uncle Tseng, a well-practised alcoholic, does not drive, and at the lake he is far from a liquor store. Zack and Till, at 3 or 10, were happy in isolated lake-side play: now their interests are more in condoms than canoes. Molly and Poldy, of course, are caught in the conventional middle. Etc., etc.

There comes, then, the crisis time, a February decision time

22 M L'Engle, *A Circle of Quiet*, Harper and Row, San Francisco, 1972, 38-9.

regarding holidays, which never before was a real decision time, bursts into a communal neurotic need to pause, to take stock, to turn to the idea, the ideas of holiday and misery, of desperations and desires.

And here I must ask of you a fantasy of optimism. The family is magnificently resilient; a lift occurs in their *notion of survival, supervivere.*[23] They shift from a plane of moral impotence, probably with the help of satire and humour, to a plane of effective and affective freedom of creative conversation.[24] The frank and discomforting issue? What has been really going on, and what is to be done about it. Remarkably, our family does not take the easy barren routes of anecdotal accusation or monadic protectiveness or groundless optimism. They structure their reflective efforts. They need, not anecdotes, but evidence: so, they dig up diaries and souvenirs, accounts of weather and neighbourhood changes, etc. Till's diaries of 15 years reveal the frustrations of blossoming feminine freedom in the presence of paternalism; uncle Tseng's jottings to a Chinatown mate show a growing horror of mere water; etc.

But the family are wise enough to consider *revealing* and *showing* to somehow be a task beyond the mere gathering of records. What might be called Research can provide the old account, the quaint shorestone: but these have to be interpreted, and the interpretation may vary greatly from family member to family member, from one age-level to another.

Further, it is one thing to talk about the meaning of this shorestone for Zack fifteen years ago: it is another task to place it in a story of Zack's 23 years. What was going on in Zack's growing up, particularly in those July holidays? What was, is, the true story of those Julys together in these decades?

23 "The Notion of Survival", where survival is taken in the superlative sense, is the title of chapter 10 of P. McShane, *Wealth of Self and Wealth of Nations: Self-Axis of The Great Ascent*, University Press of America, 1978. The treatment there complements the present discussion.
24 The context here is B. Lonergan, *Insight*, chapter 18, sections 2.6 to 3.5.

Again, you must envisage here an open struggling group, each with their own bent, putting together his or her story, each a version of their story together; the genesis of a set of histories. Which is the correct history? How might the family tackle that further, fourth, task? Surely each must mull over all the versions on a sort of discomforting dialectic tightrope.[25] Each, in that mulling struggle, seeks not just a *best account* but something basic to a future July, a set of norms, measures, for *best times together*[26], a forward-looking Foundation that itself grounds a descent towards future policy, planning, concrete decisions.[27]

So, out of Dialectics emerges, painfully, illuminatively (think of the puzzles earlier in this chapter) a Foundational view that is hard to disagree with self-consistently: genuine desires of all should not be frustrated; the desires of each are changing, growing, realities that all should advert to, attend to, but always with a reach towards the full context of change, emergence, limitations. And, strangely but not so strangely, this turn from the four tasks regarding the past generates a mirroring of those tasks in the reaching towards the future, towards July. Policy reaches for truths in a way that parallels history's search, but now they are truths that, normatively, should lace through the story as it emerges: 'We hold these truths', as the American Constitution puts it. Interpreting them adequately is another and difficult matter, task: planning must be systematic and deeply the opposite of amnesia.[28] In the light of past success and failure – itself subject to constant creative anamnesis – a spectrum of possible holidays can be hypothesized, a range of

25 The relevant strategy is described very precisely in B. Lonergan, *Method in Theology*, Herder and Herder, 1972, 245-250.
26 See *Ibid.*, 251: "presenting an idealized version of the past, something better than was the reality." This connects up with the problem of contrafactual history in economics, and its proper place among the tasks. See note 33, below.
27 *Ibid.*, 365-7.
28 I have treated this topic in "Systematics: A Language of the Heart", to appear as chapter five in McShane, *The Redress of Poise*.

which seems better than the shrinking conventions of recent years. The final step of shared strategic decision will bring that spectrum into the concrete context of present finances and weather forecasts, health and age and sickness, the give and take of an upcoming July together or perhaps not together.

I hope that, as you worked through my story, you had glimpses of where I was leading you. In its fullest scope, you could come to associate uncle Tseng, the relation by marriage, with the Chinese Ecumene which puzzled Eric Voegelin.[29] Tseng's bent towards booze, of course, has no significance, though one could think out parallels regarding oriental psychic strangeness and potentials of The Middle Kingdom frustrated by so-called Western Civilization.[30] For the 20 years you may substitute 20 centuries, or 20 million years: Grandma Moses is a bow both to remote African and proximate Hebrew origins.

My concern, then, is for the human family in its obscure Vedic reachings for a structure of reflection, education, *Wendung zur Idee*, that would raise the chances of communal well-being. The relevant present structure, I would claim, has been discovered: an eightfold structure of global *academic*[31] collaboration that meets needs desperately present in areas as seemingly separated as musicology and ecology. I myself have sketched out those needs in musicology; Arne Noess, the father of the Deep Ecology movement, has struggled with something similar in ecology. He arrives at four collaborative

---

29 Eric Voegelin, *The Ecumenic Age, Vol. 4 of Order and History*, Louisiana State University Press, 1974, the concluding sections.

30 See P. McShane, "Middle Kingdom, Middle Man. T'ien-hsia: i jen." chapter one of *Searching for Cultural Foundations*, University Press of America, 1984.

31 I write *academic* thus to recall the serious concerns of those who gathered in Academus' backyard. Such concerns stand in contrast with what is regularly meant now by the words *merely academic* – which surely says something about learned discourse. See Eric Voegelin, *Order and History, Volume 3*.

layers that correspond roughly to my four forward-looking tasks.[32] But before further comment it is best to list the eight tasks in the order in which they were described, in their correct functional order. It is an order that serves the function - you are already used to functional distinctions from our elementary analysis - of adequately searching out the meanings of the past in order, and in an order, to reach positive local decisions within a global context. Each task, in that sense, is a functional specialty, to be shared by many so disposed, globally, collaboratively, in concrete realities that range from slow mail to E-mail, journal to encyclopedia, intimate exchange to large assemblies. They relate forward towards concrete decisions, but also vortex-fashion, as the diagram that follows indicates, and also cross-collaboratively[33] in the order in which they are listed.

1. *Research*: finding relevant data, written or other.

2. *Interpretation*: reaching the meaning of such data, the meaning of those that produced it.

3. *History*: figuring out the story, connecting the meanings of the writings and the doings, etc.

4. *Dialectics*: coming up with a best story and best basic directions: recall the family problem of sorting out the different versions.

5. *Foundations*: Expressing the best fundamental (in the sense that they are not tied to age, time, etc.) directions.

32 Arne Noess, "Deep Ecology and Ultimate Premises", *The Ecologist*, Vol.18, 1988, 131. This volume includes the special double issue on deep ecology (No. 4 and 5), devoted to "Rethinking Man and Nature: Towards an Ecological Worldview". My own work on musicology is "Metamusic and Self-Meaning", chapter two of *Shaping of the Foundations*, University Press of America, 1976. An equivalent analysis of the needed division of labour in literary studies is in chapter five of P. McShane, *Lonergan's Challenge to the University and the Economy*, University Press of America, 1980.

33 The cross-collaboration can be diagrammed by an eight-by-eight matrix. So, e.g. element C_{37} represent dialogue between a historian and a systematizer. The matrix can be considered symmetric, so the dialogue represented by the element is two-way. My example gives you an opportunity to think out dialogue regarding contrafactual history. See note 13 of chapter 2.

6. *Policies*: Relevant basic pragmatic truths, somewhat like the core of national constitutions or of tribal legends.

7. *Planning-Systems*: drawing correctively and contrafactually on the strategies of the past to envisage ranges of time-ordered possibilities.

8. *Communizings*: local collaborative reflection that selects creatively from ranges of possibilities.

A diagram will help. I take it from another context, where I used a Joycean twist in the reference *the keyhole to, given*[34] and the vortex of collaboration has the appearance of a keyhole. But it still has the roundness of a wheel, thus representing the wheeling round of human experience within a *Wendung zur Idee* that reaches, not for some Platonic or Hegelian vision, but for some slight improvements in the *nomos*, the melody, the measuring of human well-being.

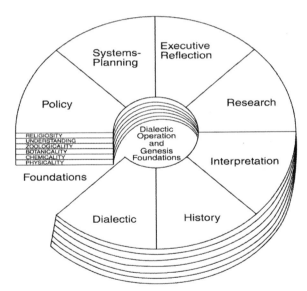

34 This diagram is one of several provided in P. McShane, *Process: Introducing Themselves to Young (Christian) Thinkers*, chapter four. It seemed best to leave it unchanged, even with the twisted reference to the conclusion of Joyce's *Finnegans Wake*, "The keys to. Given!" The task of Foundations is given a special place, since it continually reaches for an expression of the fundamental perspective that keeps the total operation rolling.

Our interest here is to see, in an introductory way, how this division of labour is needed in, and would be massively transformative of, concretely-directed economic inquiry. But we do well to pause over its significance in the context of the aspirations of The Club of Rome.

Twenty three years after its foundations it produced a report, *The First Great Global Revolution,*[35] which is divided into two parts, *The Problematique* (3 to 130) and *The Resolutique* (133 to 259). The problems are pretty evident, among them being "The International Mismanagement of the Economy" (chapter three, 74 to 95). The solution is lightweight, but contains some suggestive aspirations and slogans. "We can hope that the semi-chaos which is now taking over will eventually provide the material for a self-organizing system with new possibilities" (106). The global approach to problems as expressed by the *problematique* implies the need for a corresponding global approach at every level of society within a global perspective to interactive solutions destined to solve the problems. Therefore, a new methodology or better, a new enabling and purposeful analysis intended to be an answer to the world *problematique* is exactly what the Club of Rome means to adopt and call the world *resolutique* (135). "We see the most important task of education as learning how to learn"(210). "Today we have enormously greater amounts of information and knowledge about man and the universe than our forefathers had, but there are few signs that human wisdom has increased significantly over the last 5000 years. In these difficult and complex times we begin to realize that the pursuit of wisdom is the essential challenge that faces humanity" (218).

I cannot expect you to figure out precisely how the eightfold structured wisdom[36] proposed above meets powerfully and concretely

35 Alexander King and Bertrand Schneider, *The First Global Revolution, A Report by the Council of Rome*. Pantheon Books, New York, 1991.

36 Wisdom can be thought of as the ability to judge and to order: the troubleshooter is an instance of particular wisdom. The wisdom at stake here, however, is a total wisdom, ordering the human collaboration in the search for ontogenetic and phylogenetic order.

the needs expressed in these slogans and aspirations of the Club of Rome. In this small text I have focused on the need for a radical shift in economic thinking; here, as it were at the last minute, I have added a further focus on strategies of taking measure of economic achievement, be that achievement in theory or in the national and global management of economies. And it is quite a job to get a serious sense of the semi-chaos of economic theory and management as it is magnificently met by this *self-organizing system with new possibilities*, by this *enabling and purposeful analysis*. Your task of reflection can be greatly helped by moving your thinking, and indeed yourself, into those shelves of a university library which are inhabited by periodicals which deal with the economy. They represent a chaos of economic concern, even sometimes the mere concern to get something published, or in the case of some glossy journals, to get something sold. But, in contrast with such glossy concerns there are the lightweight journals of protest and hope, and there are the more weighty ones that still mirror larger concerns such as those expressed in Galbraith book, already cited, or in George Gilder's opposed view.[37] Then there are the standard journals, some mildly

37 JK Galbraith, *A Journey Through Economic Time*, Houghton Mifflin, New York, 1994; G Gilder, *Wealth And Poverty*, Basic Books, New York, 1981. These two books would give a nice start for an American who wished to follow up the problem of moving from different stories through dialectics to foundations. Instead of Zack and Till, we have two opposed political orientations. One must think out what would replace their very selective, aggressive, references to each other in their texts. There is too much at stake in our global turmoil to consider such popular presentations and confrontations adequate. We need a new, mediated, face to journalism. See P. McShane, *Searching for Cultural Foundations*, University Press of America, 1984, xv-xviii. The shift in journalism and popular debate requires the mediation of the eightfold strategy, but most especially the lift of serious self-discovery. This is more true, of course, of academic debate. You might take as an instance Joan Robinson's delightful little book, *Economic Heresies: Some Old-Fashioned Questions in Economic Theory*, Basic Books, New York, 1973, or indeed her entire academic life as a frustrated stand of one Cambridge against the other. The strategy of functional specialist thoroughness would certainly be an improvement of such confrontational non-dialogue. Recall also the list of problems at note 3 of chapter three. These problems are lifted out of *anecdotal treatment* by the empirical strategies sketched above. So, for example, the question of the effectiveness of a change of interest rate would be sifted through the specialties with sufficient seriousness to ground both *communizings* and a healthy journalism regarding such operations.   156

systematic, some broadly historical, some at home in third world development, some discouragingly mathematical, but all lacking the fundamental theoretic perspective towards which the present little text points. And all lacking – this is your present exercise – the massive integrative perspective of the eightfold structure suggested above. Even were the present journals on track – recall Kaldor's comment, Eichner's book, Robinson's struggles[38] – that perspective would render obsolete the scattered topic-titles and discourse of the Journal tradition much as the shift of Meyer and Mendeleev transformed chemistry journals in the 1870s. Finally, there is the recent explosion of discussion of economic method, in older journals of philosophy and in bright new journals. These are, alas, I risk claiming, cabined and confined in a truncatedness of interest that they share with Cognitive Psychology, the recently emergent so-called Critical Thinking, linguistic studies, and related disciplines. Even when they talk the language of mind – as of course, they do if they make rational choice in economics a topic – they remain cut off from mind. Most pathetic, of course, is the surge in the so-called search for mind: magnificent work made possible by such advances as magnetic resonance imaging and positron-emission tomography, radically misinterpreted. "The neglected subject does not know himself; the truncated subject not only does not know himself, but does not know that there is anything there to know."[39] For them, to continue with Lonergan, "what goes on between the input from sense and the output in language, that is obscure, vague, unconvincing. To them the human mind is just a black box. The input is clear enough. The output is clear enough. But the inner working is a mystery...

38 See notes 4 and 5 of the prologue, and note 26 of chapter one.
39 B. Lonergan, "The Subject", *A Second Collection*, Darton, Longman and Todd, 1974, 73.

My little book, *Insight*, provides a set of exercises for those that wish to find out what goes on in their own black boxes. But it is only a set of exercises. What counts is doing them. Should one attempt to do them? As long as one is content to be guided by one's commonsense, to disregard the pundits of every class whether scientific or cultural or religious, one need not learn what goes on in one's black box. But when one moves beyond the limits of commonsense competence, when one wishes to have an opinion of one's own on larger issues, then one had best know just what one is doing. Otherwise one too easily will be duped and too readily exploited."[40] It is an exploitation that is upon us, far beyond any Marxist dream of exploitation. But the reach is much more than an exclusion of exploitation. "Popularly put, you are larger than the Red Square, taller than Manhattan, deeper than galactic space. Not to contemplate that aspirative universe within is more than a sorry personal loss."[41] It is a loss objectified in all too many learned journals and artistic gests of this past century, in the tomes and towns of the nineteenth century, the encyclopedia of the enlightenment, the disputes and distresses of the Reformation, medieval decay.

But I would like to bring you on, in this exercise, from vague hints to a final illustration, to a particular shelf, and to a particular copy of what some may consider the leading economic journal, *The Economic Journal* 101 (1991). I invite you to peruse the January part, pages 1 to 155: we enter the first volume of the second hundred years of the journal, so the topic is the next hundred years of economics. Many of the authors are apologetic, none are seriously enlightening. One writer throws in a quote from Joan Robinson, on econometrics, which has not a little black humour: "We are looking in a dark room for a black cat which left before we got there" (152).

40 From a lecture entitled "Self-Transcendence: Intellectual, Moral, Religious", Lonergan delivered at Hobart and William Smith Colleges, October 10, 1974.
41 P. McShane, *Wealth of Self and Wealth of Nations*, University Press of America, 1976, Chapter 10, conclusion.

The last article, whose author is suitably named Wiseman, is suitably named 'The Black Box', and he starts well: "I must begin with a justification, if not an apology. I have long preached that mainstream economics is fundamentally flawed, not least by its inability to come to terms with the reality that the future is unknowable. How then can I accept an invitation to express a view about the state of economics a century from now?" William Baumol has the lead article with title, 'Towards A Newer Economics: The Future Lies Ahead!', and he, too, begins well: "My title is about as far as I have ever been willing to go in the way of prognostication." And in between these there are the muddles of great names. All in all, a pretty poor show, not good cricket, and certainly not baseball.

So perhaps it is time for me to come clean to you, my patient reader who has struggled this far. The difficulty of my point, indeed of my task in this text, is that what is at issue is a triple paradigm shift in economic thinking. There is, firstly, the paradigm shift of a theory of economic dynamics that definitely *crosses the Rubicon*: that has been our main topic. There is the paradigm of the eightfold structure of economic inquiry that you have glimpsed in these past few pages. But there is the more fundamental third paradigm shift, underlying the previous two and grounding the probability of their occurrences. It is a shift, against modern and post-modern truncation, towards a deep and precise plumbing of the depths and heights of human desire and imagination, the discomforting entry into one's own black box of which Lonergan writes. And it seems fitting, in conclusion, to acknowledge him clearly as the originator of all three paradigm shifts. I presume to quote from an article I finished a few days before Lonergan died, in 1984. It was meant to be celebratory of his 80th birthday, less than a month later: it emerged as an obituary.

Lonergan's economics moves more in the perspective of Cantillon and Quesnay than that of Adam Smith or Walras.

But again we must note a transposed perspective that can focus on the good of a standard of living that is concrete yet contextualized by transvalued values. There is here no labour theory of value but value as specified by a good of order within an emergent probability that measures success in strange ways. Moreover, as against abstract and centralist economic dynamics, Lonergan's analysis, mediated by procedural lucidity, focuses relentlessly on concrete possibilities and fosters individual creativity.

Causing in the human group the horizon-shift necessary to reach such a dynamic economic creativity is the massive century-long task of education of which Lonergan has written in one of his economic manuscripts: 'coming to grasp what serious education realizes, and, nonetheless, coming to accept that challenge constitutes the greatest task of the modern economy.' That grasp is the root grasp which has been our topic throughout, a grasp deeply beyond present educational efforts of theory and practice, ranging from kindergarten through Harry Stottlemeier's Discovery to the cultured truncation of graduate life.[42]

That grasp has not, indeed, been our topic throughout this short book, with its focus on the first paradigm shift. But the generation of the data has been: the emergence in your consciousness of small insights that have accumulated into the beginnings of a viewpoint. To reach the grasp in question, light in the black box, one has to turn on this viewpoint, mindpoise, to reach a viewpoint on it in its genesis and on viewpoints in their strange reality and their root possibility. Through such heart-stretching reaching you

42 The tribute to Lonergan, from which this is taken, was first published in *Compass*, 1984; it is included as Appendix 3 in P.McShane, *Process: Introducing Themselves to Young (Christian) Minders.*

can make your own small personal contribution to an optimism, a clearheaded negomodernism that can steal from post-modernism a positive affirmation: *the future is not what it was.*[43]

43 Margaret A.Rose, *The Post-Modern and The Post-Industrial: A Critical Analysis*, Cambridge University Press, 1991, 169. The reference gives me a final opportunity to note that the methodology sketched in this final chapter of our text grounds the answer to the post-modern groping for a critique of metanarratives and for the renunciation of claims to mastery. My meaning of modernity, of course, does not fit in with the narrow view of the contemporary debate described by Rose.

Epilogue

Six months of pondering the topics and the audiences that I might address in this epilogue lead me now to cling to brief descriptive indications. I must add some further words for beginners, but also there are two other definite audiences I must address: professional economists and Lonergan scholars. The range of topics calling for comment is less definite: certainly, my subtitle; but there are such issues as the role of interest rates,[1] the measurement of capital question,[2] the detailed analyses of economic flows,[3] short term and long term effects on financial institutions, legal structures, government activities.[4] My footnoting here, perhaps, gives sufficient indication of intent: comments on difficult issues are catered for there. I really see no point, at the end of my quite incomplete introduction, in condensed expression of comments by Lonergan on most of these issues, comments being published within the year. Most of these issues are concerns, not of beginners, but of professionals. I would hold that they deserve the professional attention of the eightfold dynamic which I sketched in chapter five. The problem and pseudo-possibilities of measuring capital, in particular, has generated a large technical literature: what would the value be of elaborating further on what might seem a naive view, that the technical literature struggles with increasing subtlety to swing round an evident indeterminacy,

---

1 See *CWL 15*, section 26; *CWL 21*, chapter 18, section 13.
2 See above 21, 57-58.
3 *CWL 15*, sections 26-8; *CWL 21*, chapter 18.
4 My reader must turn to the two volumes of Lonergan's economic writings for leads on these topics. Detailed references would be superfluous here, since the volumes are comprehensively indexed.

that what are determinate are prices and quantities at what I might call the faces of production. My sympathetic beginner, perhaps, sees no problem: nor, I think, is there one. But the professional, especially if she or he is out of sympathy with post-Keynesian efforts, will find it difficult to envisage the complex struggle of decades as largely beside the point.

So I turn now to address, or to reflect on, the audience of orthodox economists.

I recall my earlier quotation from Joan Robinson about first year university.[5] Robinson herself is an interesting study or example of a generous but unsuccessful effort to break beyond an education within a limiting tradition. My own experience of teaching philosophy for three decades is that humans are relatively easily disoriented. Students sometimes turned up in my classes, which focused on a self-discovery of the transcultural in human subjectivity, versed in some form of linguistic, phenomenological or existential analysis which already cut them off from serious self-attention, from attention to the relevant data. What then if one is deeply versed in some version of the Walrasian or the Keynesian tradition? If *one* is *you* then you may likely answer: my introduction is a rather vague ramble round and away from the real issues of economic analysis. I recall applying for support in this work from Canada Council in 1977. My request was turned down, and the rejection was graciously accompanied by the comment of one referee. Was it you?! "What we have here is a case of two ideosyncratic theologians trying to do ideosyncratic economics. The probability of this being fruitful is not zero, but it is not much higher."[6] So, I am left with the longterm optimism of Max Planck which pivoted on the passing of professors as permitting a new view to break through.

There is a question here of the capacity for concrete liberating fantasy, not altogether different from Progoff's cultivating daydreams

5 See above, at note 8 of chapter 1.
6 *Canada Council Research Application Files*, no. 410-78.0018.

in the stale molecules of middle age.[7] Over the past two decades I have grown in the understanding of the character of, and need for, such concrete fantasy.[8] In the present context I relate that character and need to what Lonergan remarked about *speculation* in the quotation at the end of chapter two.[9] There is the growing scandal of narrow orthodoxies, ranging from the orthodoxies of religious business to those of the highways of information and automation. Childhood imagination has been the victim of this past century – toywise and traumawise – and the victim seeds adult staleness, busy neurotic cover-stories. The urban is settled in a flow of old mobiles past the glitter of new follies and the glumness of old faiths, pumping into airwaves and country ways a busy necrophilia.[10]

At issue is human nature in its mysterious molecular vibrant finality.[11] But all this is way beyond an epilogue, an epiphanic task of artists and authors of a new millenium. So let me keep the problem in focus by holding to this small book's effort, an effort to foster concrete fantasy in what might be stalely called the methodology of economics.

What, after all, is economic methodology? Is it not simply a matter of various interlocking communities who study economic events, teach others, apply results, advise, revise, surmise? In particular, there is the community of those who think and talk about

7 Progoff's insights and strategies are of broader educational significance, but the entire field needs a fuller explanatory thematic that would integrate the chemical, the aesthetic, etc. Such a thematic is offered by Lonergan's aggreformic perspective.
8 I introduced the notion of fantasy, in a technical sense, in P. McShane, *The Shaping of the Foundations*, University Press of America, 1976, 117.
9 The final key note, number 26, of chapter two.
10 I have discussed this from a larger historical perspective in "Middle Kingdom, Middle Man: T'ien hsia; i jen", chapter one of McShane, *Searching for Cultural Foundations*, University Press of America, 1984.
11 On the obscure openness of vertical finality see B. Lonergan, "Mission and Spirit", *A Third Collection*, Paulist Press, 1988, 23-34. The context is *Insight*'s discussion of finality: see the index under *finality*.

these activities. And it is of this latter community that I think especially when I write of staleness. *Staleness* is a thin verbal pointing, a touching of the surface of a deep self-exclusion that warps the words and ways of advisors, surmisers, teachers. In the case of the subgroup, the talkers about economic talk, the so-called philosophers and methodologists, there is a dominant presence of a double neglect of data: the neglect of the given of layered economic surgings, the neglect of the surgings of creative humanness.[12] A subgroup that should be the seed of deeper creativity can become the tramp of a culture's tongue, the herd of podium and paper and parliament, the death-blood of our daze. No dangerous diseasing Socrates here, but rather the danger of a disease that is an easy mesh with 'intellectual pimps for power',[13] 'papmongers or propagandists of whatever stripe... powers windowdressers everywhere'.[14]

What I would mean, normatively, by economic methodology involves, unfortunately, the triple paradigm shift that I sketched in

---

12 There is little point in detailed reference here. The book by M. Blaug, already mentioned in chapter one, note 16, is a reasonable introduction for beginners. Philosophers may find it useful to peruse recently established journals like *Economics and Philosophy* and *Research in the History of Economic Thought and Methodology*. Economists feeling their way out of the neo-classical tradition could find it worthwhile to meet challenges from the *Journal of Post-Keynesian Economics*. A recent edition of that journal, volume 13, 1991, contains a survey and bibliography of work in methodology: Clive Beed, "Philosophy of Science and Contemporary Economics" (pages 459-495; David F. Ruccio, "Post-modernism and Economics", (pages 495-511). The problem, of course, is the established mindset. Both in philosophy and economics Joan Robinson's challenge must be met: "it is time to go back to the beginning and start again" (Robinson and Eatwell, 51). The beginning is the enquiring mind, tracking its own inventiveness.

13 Eric Voegelin, *Plato and Aristotle. Order and History*, Volume 3, Louisiana State University Press, 1957, 37.

14 S Heaney, *The Government of the Tongue*, Faber and Faber, London, 1988, 61.

chapter five. But it is, initially, you and I cajoling[15] our own molecular imagination in an upsurge of our battered curiousity about our commerce, about our curiosity. It is you and I somehow stepping aside from a soap opera of steady reading and pseudo-science that would seal and steal our souls.

One obvious *in* to that stepping aside that you would assume me to recommend is the invitation of Bernard Lonergan's writings, and before commenting further on our problems as beginners it is profitable to turn my attention to the audience that represents an already established interest in Lonergan.

My reader has already gathered that the Canadian Bernard Lonergan (1904-1984) developed an interest in economics during the late twenties, struggled with the problem privately through the thirties, and eventually produced two typescripts, one in 1942 of 133 pages and one in 1944 of 129 pages, with substantial fragments

---

15 "The first directive, then, is to begin from interest, to excite it, to use its momentum to carry things along. In other words, the method of metaphysics primarily is pedagogical: it is headed towards an end that is unknown and as yet cannot be disclosed; from the viewpoint of the pupil it proceeds by cajoling..." (*Insight*, 398). What Lonergan says here of philosophic method is, of course, true generally. In so far as generalized empirical method (see note 28, below) becomes a cultural and educational reality, methodological self-discovery will be a presence even in lower school grades. Cajoling towards a questioning and an appreciation of the human quest will become the centre of education in any sphere. Contrast this hopeful normativity with the comment on indices of books on education, child psychology, etc. in note 7 of chapter one. This simple index illustration is just one pointer towards "the monster that has stood forth in our time" (Lonergan, *Method in Theology*, Herder and Herder, New York, 1972, 40). The page continues with the contrast of vertical liberty. See note 11 above). So, I take a stand on the conviction expressed in the quotation within footnote 4 of chapter one. The shift in education that Lonergan calls for (see note 7 of chapter five, above, and the text there) is not just a shift in undergraduate economics. My epilogue notes seek to give some few pointers to the character of the shift.

marking the transition from the first to the second.[16] Lonergan scholars are, in general, no better informed regarding these efforts than the general reader: the publication of his writings on economics coincides with that of this introductory work. Students of Lonergan are, however, normally versed in Lonergan's later achievements: his work in philosophy that is brought into focus in *Insight*, his work in theology, and his further study of method, titled *Method in Theology*, an achievement, as I have noted, not restricted to theology.[17]

But now I must strike a discomforting note for Lonergan students. Lonergan was, above all else, a man who was extremely comfortable in the world of theory: which, of course, left him living in a Proustian discomfort. By *theory* here I do not mean broad scholarly activity or vague *theorizing*. I mean a world of seriously explanatory relating mightily distant either from the world of common sense or from the mentality of post-systematic and post-theoretic meanings. He took a stand on Butterfield's claim regarding the scientific revolution of the sixteenth and seventeenth centuries, that that revolution "outshines everything since the rise of Christianity and reduces the Renaissance and Reformation to the rank of mere episodes, mere internal displacements, within the system of medieval Christianity."[18]

Lonergan's presence in, and respect for, this central horizon shift of the last millennium is the hearty ethos both of his heuristics

16 The three parts of *CWL 21*, roughly of equal length, give the two texts with the bulk of the transition material between them. *CWL 15* is largely concerned with the transformations of the 1944 text that occurred when Lonergan was teaching the subject in Boston College Theology Department 1978-82.

17 *Insight* was completed in 1953, published first in 1957, and is now available as part of the Collected Works, University of Toronto Press, 1992. *Method in Theology* was completed in 1971, published first in 1972, and is now available as a paperback from University of Toronto Press, 1990. It will be Volume 12 of the Collected Works. Lonergan's work was primarily in theology. There will be about 25 volumes in the Collected Works.

18 Herbert Butterfield, *The Origins of Modern Science*, 1965, vii.

and of his castigation of the pretensions of commonsense specula-tion.[19] Regularly he noted the role of the explanatory development of the elementary science of physics in the genesis of precise self-knowledge. "Modern science had made it possible to distinguish very sharply between preliminary description and scientific expla-nation."[20] "Self-knowledge involves a self-objectification and, before man can contemplate his own nature in precise but highly difficult terms he has to bring the virtualities of that nature into the light of day... such a study would not be possible without the prior devel-opment of the sciences."[21] In his later writings he wrote regularly of three conversions: religious, moral, and intellectual. He did not write of theoretic conversion. Why? I would hold that it was because this conversion to theory was too familiar to him, too obviously a piece of cosmic development, too clearly necessary to a thinker if that thinking was to be the salt of the earth.

I could well be side-tracked here into the function theoretic conversion has as the normal mediation of intellectual conversion. The latter is the central philosophical transition to which Lonergan invites, but it is not central to my reader's interest in economics, or to my present focus.[22] That focus is still on concrete fantasy, but

19 Lonergan's view of commonsense disorientation of theoretic aspiration is briefly expressed in *Insight*, 416-421, 536-542
20 Lonergan, *Insight*, 487.
21 *Ibid.*, 535.
22 One of the signs of decadence of so-called Lonerganism is its failure to attain or even, perhaps, to suspect, the radical discontinuity of what I call extreme real-ism. It represents a massively disconcerting personal change that is initiated by "the discovery (and one has not made it yet if one has no clear memory of its startling strangeness) that there are two quite different realisms, that there is an incoherent realism, half animal and half human, that poses as a half-way house between materialism and idealism and, on the other hand, that there is an intelli-gent and reasonable realism between which and materialism the half-way house is idealism." *Insight*, xxviii = *CWL 22*. See McShane, "The Core Psychological Pres-ence of the Contemporary Theologian", *Trinification of the World*, eds. T.A. Dunne and J.M. Laporte, Regis College Press, 1978, 84-96; "General Method", chapter five of *A Brief History of Tongue*, 1998.

now more precisely in relation to the struggle towards serious understanding, in relation to serious reading.

At some stage in our adult life, if we are seriously intellectual, there must emerge the discovery that much reading, much of our previous reading, has not been at all serious. In a later stage of meaning such a discovery will be a discovery of early childhood, mediated by self-enlightened educators supported by a quest-toned culture. But to the culture of this century, in particular the subculture engaged in reading Aquinas, Lonergan found it necessary to point out what will, I hope, be evident to any educated teenager of the next millennium:

> Inasmuch as one may suppose that one already possesses a habitual understanding similar to that of Aquinas, no method or effort is needed to understand as Aquinas understood; one has simply to read, and the proper acts of understanding and meaning will follow. But one may not be ready to make that assumption on one's own behalf. Then one has to learn. Only by the slow, repetitious, circular labor of going over and over the data, by catching here a little insight and there another, by following through false leads and profiting from many mistakes, by continuous adjustments and cumulative changes of one's initial suppositions and perspectives and concepts, can one hope to attain such a development of own's own understanding as to hope to understand what Aquinas understood and meant.[23]

23 Lonergan, *Verbum. Word and Idea in Aquinas*, University of Notre Dame Press, 1967, 215-6.

And what is it to read Lonergan adequately? Later I will relate levels of adequacy to levels of authenticity and successfulness. Here let me stay with the notion of intellectual adequacy. Then, if my claim is correct, in reading Lonergan on whatever topic one is reading into the world of theory, a world that is quite beyond one if one has received some standard education in philosophy or theology. That experience of beyondness and the effort it calls for is, of course, quite familiar to anyone who has been properly taught in mathematics or physics. Then three good years of undergraduate work can render one B.A., Basically Adequate as a reader in that field.[24]

Let us pause over a particular instance of reading Lonergan, a pause that may help both the general reader and the Lonergan student.

Halfway through the book *Insight* Lonergan arrives at the statement, "let us say that explicit metaphysics is the conception, affirmation and implementation of the integral heuristic structure of proportionate being."[25] A baffling cloud of words, surely, for the beginner. Can I come up with some helpful hints? Well, whatever it is, "explicit metaphysics is a personal attainment"[26]: but of what? Of a conception, an intellectual perspective: so, to be won the same way as any other serious concept is to be won, by creative and patient curiosity. As you experienced, I hope, with the puzzle and with Pythagoras in chapter five. Or with the relations to be discovered within production and commerce.

But this conception is an altogether mightier enterprize, for it would seem to include the puzzle, and Pythagoras, and production,

24 I already comented on the introductory economics text of Gordon (see chapter one at notes 27 and 28). Its strategy is typical of other North American undergraduate texts. A type of survey is given where 'basic concepts' really represent little more than basic names. This type of introduction settles the unwary student's mind into a type of enclosure which makes the student adequate only to perpetuate, in dull – often statistics-laden or model-bent – graduate theses, the inadequate status-quo.
25 *Insight*, 391.
26 *Ibid.*, 396.

and the serious conception of them, and of everything else in our galactic globe. Wow: far out. Far out of reach? Certainly out of reach of this century: but might one not hope for such metaphysicians, foundations' persons, Ken masters and mistresses, in the next millennium?[27]

The conception includes production, because production of part of the structure of our global being. Moreover, it includes the minds of producers. Further, it includes production and the minds of producers integrally – not in isolation from the concreteness of local and global culture – and heuristically – in a fullness that anticipates, serially, possibilities and probabilities. There is an intimation here of an intertwining of content and method that must be obscure to my general reader. But a return to our chapter five puzzle helps. If you do the puzzle successfully, and reflect on that successful performance, then the approach to the next puzzle will be less dark. So, too, with economic problems and metaeconomic reflection.[28]

Further elaboration would only fuddle my beginner. The main thing to suspect is the massiveness of the challenge; then you may go on to take the measure of yourself, your pupils, your children, in relation to that challenge. Success or authenticity – our penultimate

27 My focus on the next millennium, indeed on the next million years (see the Prologue at note 2) relates to my view of the axial period of history (see note 10, above). It is not the short period (600 BC to 200 BC) of Jasper's reflections in *The Origin and Goal of History*, but a period of fragmentation and decline that stretches from the emergence of written traditions to well beyond our present times. Within that period there are occasional luminous turns to the questing subject, bubbling up with precision in Aristotle, Aquinas and Lonergan. That part of Lonergan's paradigm shift is not novel.

28 The point is made very succinctly by Lonergan: "Generalized empirical method operates on a combination of both the data of sense and the data of consciousness: it does not treat of objects without taking into account the corresponding operations of the subject; it does not treat of the subject's operations without taking into account the corresponding objects"(*A Third Collection*, Paulist Press, 1985, 141).

topic – does not depend on taking up the challenge, but on rolling towards a gathering of one's personal *nomos*. This holds true both for metaphysics and for economics. As regards the economics, you may already have arrived at the conviction that this introduction is way too difficult. And this is true, at this time. If it were contextualized by serious sympathetic undergraduate courses then you might indeed reach Basic Adequacy: but under present circumstances even a year's hard creative reading just won't get you there. Sorry about that.

Lonergan students may have here an opportunity to reconceive both the full challenge and their own challenge. First of all, it requires only moderate intelligence to follow Lonergan in struggling to accept self-luminously that understanding comes through creative imagination, that understanding is shared by exploiting that dynamic in dialogue.[29] Secondly, it requires more of an effort to carry that following into a particular field of scientific inquiry: obviously it requires competence in the field, but it requires more, for scientific inquirers at present are twisted in their orientations, their language, their achievements. Thirdly, there is the push towards the larger enterprize: that requires a daring that would reach, decade-wise, for what I have called Ken Mastery.

What of Lonergan students who lack the horizon of theory, of serious explanation? These, at present, are a large majority who have been educated in a literary, scholarly, philosophical, or theological culture. My harsh view is that, without a serious withdrawal, climbing, into some world of theory – a costly effort in today's busyness – the larger enterprize cannot be an authentic goal. It need not be a personal goal, of course: few musicians write symphonies;

29 This following of Lonergan would be no mean achievement in so far as it grounded a democratic, relatively commonsense, transformation of education. For example, in helping local children through their mathematics, chemistry, etc, I am appalled at the bulky conceptualist-nominalist texts inflicted on them. Changing the teaching of one subject in one grade could be a solid lifetime's achievement.

not many musicians are of a stature to conduct them. So, there are the more modest challenges mentioned above.[30] However, I would make two points relevant to our present context. First of all there is the dire need of a shift to a democratic minding of the economy mediated by adequate economics. A surge of interest in Lonergan's economics among his students would give a lift to the statistics of that shift. Secondly, that serious interest would in turn give a redemptive nudge to what might be called the incipient decadence of Lonerganism.[31] The central feature of that serious surge of interest would be a discomforting but revealing experience of the exhausting climb to explanation. Such an experience would lift the student to a new sympathy with the first five chapters of *Insight*, the bridge to an adequate reading of the following two chapters, to a serious explanatory appreciation of present human decline.

And I would recall my concluding chapter's indication of how the triple paradigm shift of Lonergan is an intertwined unity. Theoretical economics needs functional specialization, a cosmopolitan

---

30 There is a question here of mood, ethos. First, there is the analogy of normal science: most scientists are non-symphonic in their work, indeed are not even broadly competent, but still contribute modestly. Secondly, there is the question of the ethos of a large cultural shift, a massively discontinuous origin such as that of Lonergan. Such discontinuity eventually will generate a popular tradition, a mediated view of elderhood, science, community, common sense. There emerges, in the human group, in elite subgroups, "an aesthetic apprehension of the group's origin. The aesthetic apprehension of the group's origin and story become operative whenever the group debates, judges, evaluates, decides, or acts - and especially in a crisis"(B. Lonergan, *Topics in Education, Collected Works*, Volume 10, 1994, 230). The crisis is upon us, especially in the sophisticated commonsense overreach foisted on us by Renaissance and Enlightenment.

31 See note 22 above. Lonerganism tends to dialogue with current philosophy, a rather fruitless enterprise. The real creative dialogue is with human inquiry in developed fields. But that dialogue's fruitfulness pivots on the inner dialogue of generalized empirical method (see note 28, above). More prosaically, one cannot do philosophy of x without competence in x.

methodology reached for in the conclusion of chapter seven of *Insight*,[32] found by Lonergan in 1965.[33] Economics needs it in all its potential refinements as a developed self-correcting global collaboration of eight international sub-communities. Paradigms for such collaboration come at present from the hard sciences: think of the range of specialized chemical journals, the global reach of *Biological Abstracts*. In so far as Lonergan students pay informed attention to the economic need, they may rise to a required concrete fantasy regarding the parallel division of labour in philosophy and theology.[34]

Finally, I keep my promise to return to my humorous subtitle, *Das Jus Kapital*, that's just capital. Meshed with the humour is a range of pointers, joistings as I like to call them, with all the twists of that word.[35] There is obviously a bow to Marx here, and I would first like to recall a regular bow of Lonergan's to Marx. Always his remark was made in the context of the need for theory, for *Die Wendung zur Idee*, for withdrawal, and he would point out that Marx was just an old guy working away in the British Museum, that the trouble with the Christian community in the nineteenth century was that there was no old guy so struggling. In the twentieth century I would claim that Lonergan was an old guy struggling mightily, and with shock-

32 Chapter twenty of *Insight* returns to the topic, reaching for one specification of the qualities of cosmopolis in what I mention below as a higher justice (not to be confused with the realities of Vatican Christianity). The lower blade of the methodology can be identified with functional specialization.

33 I discuss this in some detail in "In Tune with Timely Meaning", chapter six of my forthcoming volume, *The Redress of Poise*.

34 See note 27, above. Lonergan's basic paradigm shift in philosophy and theology is functional specialization. It has as yet called out no serious committment from Lonergan scholars.

35 My twisting is not trivial. There is a need to break out of the prevailing 'stale textbook absence of author' towards concrete intersubjective reference, the molecularly making present of "the soil from which intelligence strives to leap" (Ezra Pound: "Paris Letter on Joyce's Ulysses", May 1922, published in *Pound Joyce: The Letters of Ezra Pound to James Joyce with Pounds Essays on Joyce*, edited by Forrest Read, Faber and Faber, London, 1967, 198).

ing success. I look, hopefully, to the presence, in the twenty first century, of some old gals skirting past truncated male psyches to give us the seeds of a *Gaia* movement beyond present fantasy.

My reader may already have more than a decent suspicion of the main meaning of my subtitle: driving the economy just right, so, meeting with local and global sensitivity to the surges of the two circuits, the norms of capital deepening, widening, replacement. 'Just right', then, points not to some superhuman deductive model of optimal distribution but to the humility of the ballpark efforts described in chapter five. Driving local and global economies will never be like driving a train, will always be like steering a yacht in unpredictable seas. And one does not have to call in Aristotle's view of science in potency as limited[36] to view as off the mark, or off the wall, the reach either of Catholic social teaching or of mathematical modelling for 'just right' income distribution. The genuine reach has to be one of complex large and small negotiations of unions, managements, etc, pivoting on the enlightened self-interest towards which my introduction points.

The mention of Christian teaching brings to mind a larger justice which is not beyond intelligence but is a deeper intelligence.[37] That further operative understanding would be a further enlargement of enlightened self-interest quite different from vague Christian principles of preference for the poor, from unrealistic social yearnings for equality, from philanthropies grounded in basic injustices. It is a more distant goal, a more excellent end. My little introduction has focused on the more basic justice, the more evident malices, stupidities, misdirections, misadventures associated with poor economic science.

36 See the discussion of the relevant passages of Aristotle in Lonergan, *Verbum: Word and Idea in Aquinas*, University of Notre Dame Press, 1967, 153-155.
37 The problem of continuity and discontinuity is a component of the deeper understanding. See *Insight*, 685-692. Central to the deeper understanding is a fundamental inverse insight: see Lonergan, *De Deo Trino, Pars Systematica*, Rome, 1964, 274-5.

That focus has been very precisely on the discovery of two circuits and the just balancing, nationally and internationally, of their surges. As I noted earlier,[38] quality of life was not a concern in the effort to bring you to that discovery. But undoubtedly quality of life, and the psychic and physical environment of life, must be a concern, a growing concern, of the human community. There have been recent efforts to distinguish systematically between economic growth and the growth of well-being, between GDP and GPI (the *Genuine Progress Indicator*).[39]

Such a distinction is definitely called for, and the work certainly draws attention to warped features of provincial, state, national and international accounting. But it should not be allowed to muddy the measured rhythms that are the central concern of economic theory. The measurements of both military expenditure and crime prevention, both *growth industries* of our past century, necessarily are included in economic measures. Only fools or exploitive politicians would confuse economic growth with increased human well-being.

Lonergan's paradigm shift offers an underpinning of a lift out of the psychic shrinkage of the West so eagerly exported to East and South. There are surely some few who will accept the offer symphonically, that the many might hope for a larger life of rhyme and reason.

> History says, Don't hope
> On this side of the grave.
> But then, once in a lifetime
> The longed-for tidal wave
> Of justice can rise up,
> And hope and history rhyme.[40]

38 See chapter two, above, at notes 19 and 20.
39 The Genuine Progress Indicator is discussed succinctly in Clifford Cobb, Ted Halstead and Jonathan Rowe, "If the GDP Is Up, Why is America Down?" *The Atlantic Monthly*, October, 1995, 59-74.
40 S Heaney, *The Cure of Troy, A Version of Sophocles's Philoctetes*, Faber & Faber, London, 1990, 77.

Caring for Coloured Wholes
Operation *WHALE*

Editor's Conclusion

Chapter five in the first volume of our series ends on a gloomy note regarding Lonerganism, and there may well be a further personal gloom generated by the chapter: this Joycean-Lonergan self-searching is not really your scene, your cup of Proustean tea. Operation *WHALE* offers a turn-around to both glooms. Obviously, I must write briefly and plainly here. The focus of this concluding concern, then, is your personal perspective on global hunger and Lonergan's economics.

One cannot go far in an analysis of global annual income per individual without sensing the horror of massive disparity. Images, maps, help. Atlases can display averages over coloured wholes of countries, regularly going from darker colours of abundance, from deep red average yearly income of twenty American dollars, to the pale reality of land masses below a dollar a day. That pale reality can become skin-tied only through surges of senseability's contemplative reachings guided by books, maps, numbers, anecdotes, struggling friends. An image I cling to is that of women of India, in the present century and in eighteenth century Rajastan, clinging to trees, challenging loggers.[1] And numbers follow images: 40,000,000 non-Hindu people, 5% of India's population, will lose

---

1 On this and its relation to the Chipko (*clinging*) movement, see Robin Jeffrey. *What's Happening to India? Punjab, Ethnic Conflict, Mrs Gandhi's Death and the Test of Federalism*, Macmillan, 1986, conclusion.

their forest homes in these next decades. There is no end to such images, maps, anecdotes, in a growing literature and in the media-mesh.

At the end of one such work[2] Susan George faces my issue: "Conclusion: What We Can Do." One section is titled, "Making People-to-People Connections," and that title might well be used to describe *WHALE*. But we need reference to the discomforting diagram at note 27 of chapter four of a *Brief History of Tongue*. Where Susan George's focus is, in the main, below the central line, my focus is on the people-to-people connections represented by the complexities above the line, briefly mentioned in the editor's introduction, sketched for linguistics in chapter three. Again, the concluding part of *Africa's Choices. After Thirty Years of the World Bank*,[3] by Michael Barratt Brown, bears the title "A Framework for Cooperation," but the framework lacks the global caring of the framework I desire: it, too, deals largely with, as he puts it, "cooperation on the ground," lying outside what the diagram indicates as a transnational matrix of eight collaboration groups. But that *outside* is where the crying needs[4] are to be most efficiently met.

The word *efficiently* is key here. Lonergan's first focus was on efficiency: how to save capitalism's workers from starvation, how to move the globe towards Christ. But, no more than Plato or Thomas or Marx, did he pin down a contemporary efficient strategy. So, in *Insight*, both *cosmopolis* and *implementation* are left hanging. His eightfold way of 1965 is his giant contribution to humanity's

2 Jon Bennett with Susan George, *The Hunger Machine*, Basil Blackwell, 1987.
3 Penguin Books, 1995. This and the previous book would help the reader to sense the grim reality and the warped economics of the hungry fifth of our human group.
4 *Needs*, of course, are best thought of in the context of *Method in Theology*, 48, 286-7.

task of efficient collaboration. I insist on this economic fact in my Introduction to *For A New Political Economy*. Without this collaboration, Lonergan's foundational contribution to economic science will make headway only by random skirmishes with scheme-locked economic establishments and by slow grassroots ferment. Furthermore, what I say of Lonergan's economics is true of Lonergan's works in general. The gloom of the end of chapter five is grounded in the sad reality of Lonerganism's inefficient skirmishes mainly with established schemes of philosophy and theology meshed with grassroots advertences. Lonergan's central life searching was to finally arrive at "a practical theory of history"[5] that would give a home to culture and to all types of minders, addicts of detail, system-builders, policy-makers, marketers of meaning, whatever. It is the home that I wish to call *hodic studies*, just as chemistry's home or biology's home may be called periodic studies.[6] I select hodic as the focal adjective because it moves back from method to an Indoeuropean root. There are all sorts of suggestive linguistic resonances and cousins to the root *hod*, but my previous aligning of *Method in Theology* with *Finnegans Wake*[7] may lead you to twinkle over the line from the Wakesong, "And to rise in the world he carried a hod."

Method in Theology is a failure as a foundational work, but in its descriptive success it can be seen as a clear policy statement, *methodological doctrine*.[8] It invites each to contribute hodically – adverting, then, to one's small job within the eightfold scheme – to the rolling

---

5 *Insight*, 233 = *CWL* 3, 258.

6 Chemistry has the periodic table as mindbent. The heuristics of biology are much more complex: there are periods of evolution, but there are also genetic periods within the organism. The latter periods are a prime analogue for the genetic sytstematics of the seventh hodic specialty.

7 The parallel is developed in McShane, "Metamusic and Self-Meaning", chapter two of *The Shaping of the Foundations*, University Press of America, 1976.

8 *Method in Theology*, 295. The character and circumstances of the failure will be a central topic in B. Anderson and P. McShane, *Wealth of Nations: Of the Division of Labour in Minding*, Axial Press, forthcoming.

stone of *nomos* and progress. And what hodic studies especially needs now, in the issue of economics and world hunger, is a shift of focus from a vague tonality of retrieval to precise collaborative work on global and local policies, systems-planning, analyses of the marketing of meaning. There is a need, then, in Lonerganism, to break out of inert and conventional recurrence-schemes of retrieval – distorted shadows of the authentic dialectic sketched on page 250 of *Method in Theology* – and to move towards the personal genesis of ever-fuller foundational, doctrinal, systematic and locally analytic endeavours that would back up the reach towards tongues and tummies in the trenches of seedings and journalisms, class-texts and curricula, lobbyings and loans.

Perhaps this little book will help you to find your own frame of reference within that global scheme, to glimpse the need to escape some rut of convention that has tied you to the non-hodic retrieval of, say, the opinions of dead Europeans, even to find your way out of Lonergan studies to the trenches. But in so far as you take human hunger to heart, you will be sharing in a bent that Lonergan carried from his early days to his last years. I have spent some weeks now working through his books of those final years, following up his marginal markings, mainly to find leads on where he might have gone in thinking out an operable normative theory of interest and credit,[9] but also to catch his mood. In his copy of a book by Joan Robinson, probably read in his 76th year, two marked passages on page 34 are worth quoting.

> Economists generally seem to support the capitalists' principle that what is profitable is right. The application of this

9 I mentioned the possibility in note 24 of my Introduction to B. Lonergan, *For A New Political Theology*, University of Toronto Press, 1998. Markings in Lonergan's copy of Schumpeter's *Theory of Economic Development* confirm my suspicions. There are parallel discussions in Schumpeter's two-volume *Business Cycles*, but there is, unfortunately, no copy of it in Lonergan's last library.

principle in the Third World leads to a large part of whatever surplus is available being devoted to the kind of
production least propitious to all-round economic
progress. ... In fact, the highest level of luxurious living is
often found in the poorest countries and, with it, the greatest concentration of power in the hands of a few.[10]

He was still within the struggle of his early years, looking
towards changes which he expressed so eloquently when he was
38, when he envisioned an enlightened economist in every village,

nor is it impossible that further developments in science
should make small units self-sufficient on an ultramodern
standard of living to eliminate commerce and industry, to
transform agriculture into a superchemistry, to clear away finance and even money, to make economic solidarity a memory,
and power over nature the only difference between high civilization and primitive gardening. But we are not there yet.
And for society to progress towards that or any other goal it
must fulfil one condition. It cannot be a titanothere, a beast
with a three-ton body and a ten-ounce brain. It must not
direct its main effort to the ordinary final product of standard
of living but to the overhead product of cultural implements.
It must not glory in its widening, in adding industry to industry, and feeding the soul of man with an abundant
demand for labor. It must glory in its deepening, in the pure
deepening that adds to aggregate leisure, to liberate many

10 Joan Robinson, *Aspects of Development and Underdevelopment*, Cambridge University Press, 1979. Like the books mentioned in notes 2 and 3 above, there is a
concluding chapter on "What Now?" ending with the sad sentence, "All that
economic analysis can hope to contribute is to remove some illusions and to help
whoever is ruling to look to see what their situation really is." The book is solid
evidence of the need for the layered collaboration of which I write.

entirely and all increasingly to the field of cultural activities. It must not boast of science on the ground that science fills its belly. It must not glue its nose to the single track of this or that department. It must lift its eyes more and more to the more general and the more difficult fields of speculation, for it is from them that it has to derive the delicate compound of unity and freedom in which alone progress can be born, struggle, and win through.[11]

At that same age he concluded an article, to be published in *Theological Studies* in 1943, with an appeal: "If I have succeeded in hitting upon some pivotal points, perhaps I may hope that this labour will merit the scrutiny, the corrections, and the developments of others."[12] His hope was not fulfilled. Lonergan's explanatory perspective on marriage and mating had no serious impact on the ferment surrounding later papal and theological foolishness. Might I hope against hope that what I consider pivotal points regarding the larger mating and marriage of minding and marketing would catch critical concern?

It seems fitting to conclude where I began in chapter one, with a letter-sequence puzzle.[13] But you may have caught on much earlier to the origin of my operations title, *WHALE...* ?

11 B. Lonergan, *For A New Political Economy*, University of Toronto Press, 1998, part 1, section 9.
12. B. Lonergan, *Collection*, "Finality, Love, Marriage", conclusion.
13. The reference is to chapter one of McShane, *A Brief History of Tongue*, where this editorial conclusion first appeared. That book supplements the present one in its invitation to a personal and communal fostering of creativity.

PHILIP MCSHANE, Professor Emeritus at Mount St Vincent University, Canada, a mathematician & philosopher, has been working on economics since 1968, when he began studying Bernard Lonergan's early (1942 to 1944) economic writings. He has edited these writings in *For A New Political Economy*, University of Toronto Press, 1999. His other writings on economics include *Wealth of Self & Wealth of Nations*, 1974 and *Lonergan's Challenge to The University & The Economy*, 1980. Recently he has been lecturing on economics at universities in Mexico, Columbia, USA, Canada, Ireland, and the UK. He is directing research projects on the relation between economic theory and law, education, environmental problems, world hunger.

Other Books in The Transaxial Series

Philip McShane, *A Brief History of Tongue: From Big Bang to Coloured Wholes*, 1998